The 'Son of Sam' and Me

THE TRUTH ABOUT WHY I WASN'T SHOT BY DAVID BERKOWITZ

CARL DENARO
WITH BRIAN WHITNEY

WILDBLUE
PRESS

WildBluePress.com

'THE SON OF SAM' AND ME published by:
WILDBLUE PRESS
P.O. Box 102440
Denver, Colorado 80250

WILDBLUE PRESS is registered at the U.S. Patent and Trademark Offices.

ISBN 978-1-952225-53-6 Trade Paperback

ISBN 978-1-952225-52-9 eBook

Cover design © 2021 WildBlue Press. All rights reserved.

Interior Formatting/Book Cover Design by Elijah Toten
www.totencreative.com

The 'Son of Sam' and Me

Table of Contents

Prologue

Thanks for purchasing my book.

As you read on, you will see many details of the Son of Sam attacks that were ignored by law enforcement professionals and will read new information and updates on alternate suspects. Still, this is not an attempt on my part to finish Maury Terry's *The Ultimate Evil.*

This book is about my quest to figure out who shot me, and who, other than David Berkowitz, was responsible for the Son of Sam shootings. But this is also my story of how I was unwillingly thrust into one of the biggest cases in New York City history when I became a victim of an unknown shooter. It is also a glimpse into my 44 years as a Son of Sam Survivor and the story of my relationship with my friend Maury Terry, as well as how I began investigating this case with him and where that investigation stands now.

It is important to note that the theories espoused in this book are mine, Maury Terry's, or a combination of both. I certainly feel my theories are correct, but you be the judge. When names of suspects are used, many are pseudonyms. The exceptions to this are suspects that have been previously named in *The Ultimate Evil.*

I have to give credit to my amazing daughter, Casey, for starting me on the long road to write my book. When Casey was in her senior year as a film student at Brooklyn College, she was required to produce a student thesis film. She had started writing a script in 2015 which was based on a period of my life in 1976. Her short film, "CARL" depicted the night I was shot through the next six months when the NYPD announced that a serial killer was on the loose and then discovered that in actuality my shooting was not random at all. Casey wrote and directed "CARL" which went on to win awards at film festivals including *NY Women in Film* and the *TV Emerging Female Filmmaker* award as well as receiving a Student Grant from the National Board of Review.

While preparing to write the script, she interviewed me, friends of mine, and family members to get a true feeling of the events that changed my life. During the extensive interview process, Casey asked questions that were never posed to me in the past and I never really gave much thought to. By the time she was done, I realized that I had to write my story, even if it was just for my own piece of mind.

Casey paid for a couple of writing classes and I was on my way. Well, I quickly found out that writing a book was a lot more difficult than writing a 3.000 word story. Author Brian Whitney came on board and saved the day. Together I think we have crafted a very compelling book.

Before you begin reading, I want to assure you I am not attempting to give you a hard sell on the conspiracy angle of this case. In this book, I tried to lay out the facts as they unfolded initially as reported in newscasts and newspapers in 1977. Then I introduced evidence that was missed or ignored during the initial investigation along with circumstantial evidence that was uncovered in the years after the case was closed.

Believe me, my life would have been a lot less complicated if the simple truth was that I was in the wrong place at the wrong time and I was shot by a serial killer named David Berkowitz. I could live with that and would have no need to spend 30-plus years investigating the nagging questions, ignored evidence, and way too many coincidences that I have been left to deal with.

The conspiracy angle of the case first kicked into high gear for me when I read Maury Terry's book, *The Ultimate Evil*. As I became close to Maury and delved into the case a few years after reading the book, I realized Maury really nailed that aspect of this story. But there are issues with the book. I have come to learn, following Maury's unfortunate passing, that he sometimes stretched the truth, made some assumptions seem like fact and in some cases fabricated stories to "connect the dots."

These days the term "conspiracy theory" is often used as a pejorative. I want to share two quotes from members of The Official Maury Terry – "The Ultimate Evil" – Son of Sam & Beyond Facebook group regarding conspiracy theories.

The first is from the late Joe DiToma , author of *The Cult of the Black Sun*, who wrote this statement:

"The term conspiracy theorist was first coined in its popular form by Richard Nixon to denigrate his growing number of detractors. It is based on the belief that giving a mocking name to a phenomenon will disparage it. The investigation into occult groups was similarly disparaged with the moniker of "satanic panic."

Parris Mitchell Mayhew, who is a founding member of the legendary band, Cro-Mags, and currently a camera operator and video producer also posted his thoughts on conspiracy theories:

"The general public believes the myth supplied by the media. If someone is sufficiently predisposed to disbelieve something because they already believe they know the truth, then no facts will sway them. And of course, the carefully manufactured historical bias against any "conspiracy theory" is a knee jerk reaction to any alternate telling of events despite the thorough and meticulous research and presentation in *The Ultimate Evil*. People are sheep."

I hope you enjoy the book and encourage you to draw your own conclusions. The fact that no law enforcement officials will speak out in public about the existence of other suspects, even though many do so off the record, and there are no crime scene police reports to review has certainly muddied the waters. Wading through 45 years of missing evidence, following up on promising leads that go nowhere and the press perpetuating the "talking dog" lone gunman scenario, has made getting the facts out to the general public a daunting task.

When you finish the book, I am hoping you will believe at the very least more than one shooter was involved in the Son of Sam attacks. You will read about many instances of coincidences and circumstantial evidence that hopefully will make it difficult for you to think anything other than more than one person was involved in these shootings besides David Berkowitz.

By themselves, maybe the circumstantial evidence and coincidences can be explained away as just that, coincidences, but when you put them all together it makes for a very compelling case of conspiracy. The many police sketches that look like different people, the differing accuracy of the shooters, the varying time of the attacks, and the inconsistent M.O. of the shooters is just the tip of the iceberg.

One

Some nights, nothing much happens. Other nights change your whole life.

It was Friday night, October 22nd, 1976. It was a big occasion for me, the last evening before I left home to join the Air Force. It was also the night I was shot in the head.

I only had five more days to go until I was off to boot camp in Fort Lackland, Texas. I was hoping to have one last wild night out on the town with my friends. I met my buddies at my usual watering hole in Flushing, Peck's Depot Bar and Grill. We stayed there for an hour or so, having some drinks and joking around, then my friend Marty told us about a house party he knew of that was supposed to be hopping. I figured that would be a lot more fun than hanging out at the bar playing foosball and listening to the jukebox, so we headed over. But when we got to the party, it wasn't much better than the scene we had just left.

The evening was bittersweet. I only had a few of these wild nights left to spend with my friends before I left Queens, maybe for good. I had dropped out of college; it just wasn't for me. I then worked a series of menial jobs. Those weren't for me either. It was time to do something different. I needed to shake things up a little. But that didn't mean I wasn't going to miss my old life.

This wasn't an easy decision for me and was one I thought long and hard about. For a long-haired, pot-smoking, self-proclaimed hippie like myself, joining the military was a major move and was definitely out of character. No one I knew could believe it. But I needed a change.

It took me a few weeks to build up the courage to walk into the USAF recruitment center in Flushing, New York, but eventually I strolled into the office with all the confidence I could muster up. There I was, dressed like I was going to an Allman Brothers concert, wearing construction boots, jeans, and a flannel shirt with hair down to my shoulders, being interviewed by a square-jawed, six-foot officer in full uniform with a crew cut.

The very first question he asked me was "Why do you want to join the United States Air Force, son?"

I was stumped. The thing is, I wasn't sure. I knew it probably wouldn't be acceptable to say I was a college dropout that hated my job, that I was looking for some direction in life, or that I had no idea what else I would do.

I decided to pull out the family tradition card. I said "Well, my uncle was in the Air Force and I thought it would be a good idea to follow in his footsteps." While the latter part of this wasn't true, it seemed to be an acceptable enough answer to him, and the process continued.

I filled out some paperwork and he gave me a package to take home so I could complete the rest of the application on my own time. Once I got that in order, the next step was to take a series of tests, presumably to see what made me tick, what kind of general knowledge I had, and what type of job would be best suited for me.

Apparently, I did well on all of the tests because when the results came back, I had my choice of jobs and I opted to be an aerial photographer. My training was to begin in Colorado Springs as soon as I completed bootcamp.

I was nervous, but excited. I took a trip to Fort Greene in Brooklyn to complete an eye test and a physical exam. If all went well, I would be sworn in on that same day. I aced them both. While I waited for the swearing in ceremony, I was informed that I was eligible for a delayed entry program which gave me almost two months before I had to report to boot camp. This was cool with me, I was doing something to change my life for the better, but I still had a couple months to bum around, drinking, smoking, and partying.

Which were exactly the things I was doing that Friday night in October. The party was not as fun or as crowded as what we thought it would be, so we left and headed back to Pecks. When we got to the bar, it was starting to fill up, like it always was late on a Friday night. The Allman Brothers' "One Way Out" was blaring from the jukebox and the usual crowd was there, drinking and having a good time, including a couple of girls I knew from Queensborough Community College. I had gone out with one of them, Rosemary Keenan, a few times. She was a nice girl, really attractive, and we seemed to have some chemistry, so I was happy to see her.

She and I started talking and flirting a bit. I ordered a beer and a shot of Jack Daniels for myself and a beer for her. Rosemary and I finished our drinks and played a game of foosball then ordered another round. I was still talking and joking with the rest of the crew, but at this point my eyes were on Rosemary. Soon we broke off from our crowd and spent some time just focusing on each other.

It wasn't long before we decided to leave the bar. This was my last Friday in town after all, which meant it was my last chance with Rosemary. We got into her blue 1970 Volkswagen Beetle, she revved the engine and we drove off with no particular destination in mind. We wound up heading down 159th Street and, as we approached 33nd Avenue, I suggested she park at a spot about 25 feet from the corner in front of a large house. She glided the Bug towards the curb and turned the ignition off.

As soon as we pulled over, I took a bottle of Jack Daniels out of my pocket and took a big swig. Before long, the two of us were making out. I don't remember if we were still kissing each other when my world changed forever.

The windows of the VW exploded around me while glass sprayed over the interior of the car. I looked down and saw my hands were bleeding, filled with tiny shards of glass, gleaming in the dim light. I had no idea what happened. I didn't recall hearing a gun go off. In fact, I wasn't even aware that I was shot but, there was one thing I knew. We were in trouble.

Frantically, I yelled at Rosemary, "Start the car, let's get out of here'!" I didn't have to tell her twice. As Rosemary turned the key in the ignition, for some reason that I would soon come to regret, I took a bag of about an ounce of weed out of my pocket and threw it out the window.

As we headed down 159th Street I must have passed out. I came to about 15 seconds later and saw that Rosemary was in a panic. She didn't know where she was or where to go. Rosemary lived at home with family in Bayside and wasn't familiar with my Flushing neighbourhood. For some reason that still isn't clear to me, I told her to go back to Peck's. Obviously, directing her to Flushing Hospital Emergency room would have been a better choice, but let's just say I wasn't thinking straight. Obviously, neither was Rosemary. Soon, there we were, right back at the bar.

When Rosemary pulled up in front of the bar entrance, I got out of the car and walked in like I owned the place. Vinny, the bouncer, looked at me strangely and said, "Carl, you don't look too good."

I didn't know it then, but that was a huge understatement. "Vinny, I don't feel too good, I think the car exploded," I replied.

He pulled up a chair and sat me down. I started to feel dizzy and my head nodded down like a junkie. My shirt turned a sickening red as blood spilled down my shirt. My long hair had been sopping up the blood from my head wound. As I looked around the room, forty or so bar patrons looked back at me, staring in horror and disbelief. Nobody knew what happened, but everyone knew I needed to go to the emergency room and not be hanging out at the bar with blood gushing out of my head.

My two best friends, Bob and Marty, jumped into action and helped me to Bob's car. We raced to Flushing Memorial Hospital. To this day, none of us remember which one drove, but I know it wasn't me.

Despite my head wound, I walked into the emergency room under my own power. The medical staff immediately put me on a gurney, took me to an examination room and started working on me. I was conscious of my surroundings and wasn't feeling any pain. My adrenaline was in overdrive, hiding the fact that I was critically wounded.

Unbeknownst to me, as I laid on my stomach, the doctors had begun to take glass and bullet fragments out of the back of my head. Every time a nurse or orderly would come in or out of the examination room I waved to my friends whom I could see in the waiting room as the swinging doors opened and shut.

NYPD dispatched a homicide detective, Marlin Hopkins, to Flushing Hospital to investigate the shooting, thinking it was possible I was dead because of the report of a victim being shot in the head. But, luckily for me, I wasn't in need of a homicide detective's services. When he spoke with the attending doctor and asked what the prognosis was, the doctor assured him that I was stabilized and should make it through. Being a homicide detective, Hopkins did an about face and exited the room.

This wasn't Hopkins' only brush with the Son of Sam case. Five months after he responded to the false alarm at Flushing Hospital, he became the lead investigating detective in a homicide in Forest Hills; the shooting of Christine Freund, the fourth Son of Sam fatality.

Forty years later, I had the occasion to meet Marlin Hopkins and he told me this story about how we almost met that night in the hospital. As you can imagine he was a little reluctant to tell me he saw me on a gurney, with a hole in the back of my skull and left without as much of a hello after he was told by the doctors I would survive.

At about 4 in the morning, an NYPD patrolman in full uniform approached me. I was still lying stomach down on the gurney. He pulled up a chair next to me and sat down.

Our faces were about 12 inches apart as he looked at me and asked me a question. "Should I call your parents and let them know what happened to you?"

I started to answer that my dad lived upstate in Middletown and not with me so not to worry about contacting him, but then I stopped and asked the cop a question, "What time is it?"

When he told me, it was about 4:00 A.M., I continued. "No, don't worry about it, as long as I'm home by 7:00 in the morning my mother won't even know I was out this late."

He looked confused, wrinkled up his face and said to me, "Son, you're not going home. You were shot in the head."

This was my first indication that my injuries were caused by a bullet. No one had told me. I knew the car didn't really explode, but still, it was too much to imagine that someone had actually shot me as I was making out with Rosemary. It was just too surreal. It wasn't until a couple of days later, while still in the hospital, that I learned that there was a hole the size of a Kennedy half-dollar in the back of my skull.

Once the emergency room doctors had finished with me, I was wheeled down a long hallway and left in front of a door that read "X-RAY Room." As I lay alone in this hallway, I started to feel sick. Really sick. Before I knew it, I was throwing up fluorescent green bile and began to freak out. Soon a door opened, and an X-Ray technician came up and assured me that I was going to be okay. I wasn't sure if I believed him. After the staff cleaned me up a bit, I was wheeled into the room and the technician had me sit on the side of the gurney.

He began to put cold, hard, metal plates against the back, top, and side of my head while taking x-rays. This was precisely the time my adrenaline decided to abandon me. I developed a headache that was so severe I passed out. The next thing I knew, I woke up in a hospital room with five other patients with my head wrapped in about a hundred miles of gauze, a splitting headache pulsating through me.

How did this happen to me? There seemed to be no possible reason. I was a fun-loving jokester with a hippie attitude. A 6-foot-tall, 145-pound bag of bones with brown hair down to my shoulders, never looking for a fight, just looking for the next concert, party, or joint. And someone shot me while I was making out with Rosemary in her car? It made no sense.

I had no enemies I could think of. It was ridiculous to think someone might want to try and kill me. Especially in that manner. There was nothing in my past that would indicate I would be the target of a gunman.

Between dealing with an incredibly painful headache, coming to the realization that I was shot in the head, and wondering who would want to shoot me, I really wasn't in the meet and greet mode. I just wanted to be left alone and stew in my misery.

But I soon had visitors, nonetheless. A nurse told me that a pair of detectives had come to see me.

Two men dressed in suits strode with purpose into the six-bed ward. As they approached, I recognized a somewhat familiar face. It was none other than Rosemary's father, who just happened to be a police officer, Detective Redmond Keenan. It was painfully obvious by his demeanour that he wasn't too happy that I had been hanging out with his daughter in her car let alone her getting shot while she was with me. Things were going from bad to worse. The other officer introduced himself to me as Detective Blueze.

Awkwardly, Detective Keenan asked how I was feeling. He then asked me a lot of questions but the gist of all of them were the same, "Where did the shooting occur and who shot you?"

I told them I had no idea who shot me. I didn't even know I *was* shot until the NYPD cop told me. As far as where it happened, I was pretty sure Rosemary and I parked close to the intersection of 160th street and 33rd Avenue. I didn't have much more info to give them, so the interrogation was short and to the point. The whole thing was a blur.

Almost 40 years after this encounter with Detective Keenan and Detective Blueze, one of the bartenders who was working that night at Peck's Depot Grill told me that right after we left for the hospital, he called Rosemary's father at about 2 in the morning and told him to come pick up his daughter at the bar. Rosemary wasn't hurt so she didn't have to go to the hospital with me. The bartender told Keenan he not only had to come down to the bar and pick up his daughter, but her car was inoperable because the windows were blown out. Apparently, once Detective Keenan brought his daughter home and got the car towed, he went right to work on the crime.

If Keenan wasn't happy the first time he saw me, he was even less happy when he saw me next. A few hours later, the two detectives came back to my ward, marched up to my bed, and threatened to arrest me if I didn't tell them the truth about where I was shot. They said they went from 160th street all the way to 172nd street and didn't find any evidence of the shooting. That gave my memory a jolt and I realized we were on 159th street not 160th street. Being the smartass I was, I told them that I threw a bag of pot out of the window as Rosemary gunned the car away from the scene and told him maybe they would have better luck finding that instead. This was probably not the smartest thing to say at the time.

A few hours later, Detectives Blueze and Keenen returned to my room once again. They found the glass shards from the VW on 159th about 25 feet from 33rd Ave. A few days later it dawned on me that they went 12 blocks in one direction to look for evidence but never thought to go one block in the opposite direction. This may have seemed to be a small mistake, but it turned out this was just the beginning of what would turn out to be a flawed investigation.

I spent three weeks in the hospital recuperating from my wound. It wasn't long before everyone I knew was aware of what happened to me. This type of news travelled fast in my social circle. Within a few days' time, friends, acquaintances, and some people I didn't even know were coming to the hospital to see me.

On the fifth day of my hospital stay, my mother walked into my room and flipped out. There were close to twenty people surrounding my bed. She told everyone to get out and informed the nurses and the administration they were to ban all visitors from now on. I was happy that she got all the gawkers out, but Rosemary and my friends were fun to have around. I was in no condition to be entertaining but it was still nice to see some familiar faces. My life quickly became very lonely.

The only person outside of my family who saw me at that period of my life was one of my buddies, Bob O'Neill, who worked as an orderly in the hospital. He spent time with me whenever he could, something I very much appreciated at the time. When my U.S. Air Force report date of October 23, 1976 came, my mother contacted them and explained the situation. The Air Force had no need for a recruit with a hole in his head to report to basic training. I was given an honourable discharge but received no benefits. Armed Forced benefits are calculated only by active duty time served. At least I had a fancy USAF Honourable Discharge certificate to hang on my wall.

Most of the three-week recuperation time in the hospital was spent having my blood drawn, taking two aspirins every six hours and having fluid drained from my head. Other than that, I just sat around and stared at the walls. The fluid draining was exactly as bad as it sounds. Every three or four days, Dr. Juan Negron and a nurse came in with a huge needle and drew built-up fluid from my skull. I have to say, as bored as I became, I was never happy seeing those two walk into my room.

Finally, Dr. Negron gave the ok for me to be discharged from the hospital. Initially I was thrilled until I was told that I had to remain at home with no visitors and very little contact with people, including my family. When they took off the gauze wrapping my head, Dr. Negron explained to me only a thin layer of skin was protecting my brain from harm. Even though I was out of the hospital, I was still at risk. As bored as I was going to be, safety was of the utmost importance. It wouldn't take much to put my life in danger.

An operation was scheduled to insert a metal plate to safeguard my brain from what could be a catastrophic injury, but it couldn't be performed until the swelling in my skull went down and the open wound healed naturally. This was going to take some time. I was looking at 65 days of homebound prison.

To my dismay, a few days into my home quarantine, Detectives Keenan and Blueze made a house call. In the past four weeks, they had developed a theory that the shooting was the result of a drug deal gone awry and that the perpetrator was someone I knew. This wasn't even close to the truth, but I couldn't really blame them. It wasn't like I had any idea who shot me, and it made no sense to anyone that a total stranger shot me just for fun. And of course, there was the fact I told them about the ounce of weed.

They handed me a piece of paper with close to a hundred names on it, all of whom they considered to be potential suspects. I immediately recognized a few of them but I explained to the detectives that while I knew a lot of people, I didn't consider any of them capable of trying to kill me. Not to mention the fact none of them had a reason to. I hadn't done anyone bad enough for any of them to want me dead, not even close. Not only that, but most of them were guys who were arrested for things like stealing bikes, public intoxication, and possession of marijuana. They weren't exactly a bunch of major criminals.

Still, the detectives were positive that the shooting was the result of a drug deal and that I knew who the person was who shot me. They thought I was holding back on them and pushed me to name some of those on the list as potential shooters, but I refused. Why would I get someone in trouble I knew had done nothing wrong? I was sure the people I knew from the suspect list didn't shoot me, or maybe I just hoped that. It was too bizarre for me to think anyone I knew wanted me dead.

I didn't have an answer to give them, but I knew for a fact the story they were going with was wrong. There was no drug deal going on, and I didn't know who shot me. It was as simple as that.

Looking back, I guess I couldn't blame them. My crack at the hospital about the weed I threw out the window probably didn't help. Nor did it help I had a whole ounce of it on me. My lifestyle and my long hair all contributed to the profile of the crime they came up with. Random shootings didn't happen much in my area. Although much of New York City was under siege from shootings and robberies, my neighbourhood was almost totally insulated from the madness that was going on in Brooklyn, Manhattan, and the Bronx.

My mother wasn't a huge help either. Her response to this line of questioning was that if the shooting was a result of a drug deal, it definitely had something to do with all of the hooligans I hung out with. I couldn't believe that after being shot in the head by a stranger for no discernible reason, I had to defend myself to the detectives as well as my mother. It was a lonely and frustrating time.

While the police were way off, they didn't seem to even consider other options. At the time I was pretty critical of the police department, especially Detectives Keenan and Blueze. I mean, I got it. The detective's daughter was hanging out with a long-haired, pot-smoking hippie and she got shot at while making out in her car, but at the time I wasn't really thinking too deeply into their concerns. Law enforcement personnel that I met 20 years later were shocked when I told them Rosemary's father was assigned the case. It was highly irregular for the NYPD to assign a detective to a case that involves a family member. I can say for certain that it hindered the investigation.

The police had little contact with me after they showed me their list of suspects. Although they left me alone, Detective Keenan and Detective Blueze continued to make weekly pilgrimages to Peck's Depot Grill to ask the patrons if they saw anything strange that night. They questioned everybody that knew me about what kind of guy I was and if I had any enemies. The response was pretty much the same. I could be sarcastic and occasionally could get under someone's skin, but no one thought anyone would want to shoot me. They questioned people to see if I was involved with drug dealing. The answer to this was also no. I smoked a lot of weed back then but I never dealt it, and the guys I bought it from were strictly small time.

Days went by slowly. I found myself sitting in my mother's living room staring out the sliding glass doors watching the world go by for hours. My relationship with my mother was at best cordial even during good times. While she loved me as her son, she was not thrilled with my lifestyle and believed my shooting was a direct consequence of that. This was new territory for me. I hadn't spent a whole lot of time hanging out with my mother for the past three years. She did her best to make me comfortable and made sure that my brother and sisters didn't bother me, but things were awkward to say the least.

Sitting around the house was doing nothing for my mental health. I was consumed with fear, guilt, and questions. I couldn't get my mind to shut off. As much as I believed I didn't know my shooter, I was still nervous he would come back to finish the job. Why did he shoot me anyway? Was there actually a reason? Maybe I did do something to warrant the shooting. Did my sarcastic sense of humour do me in? Was someone pissed at me that I didn't even know about? I worried about my shattered plans to join the Air Force and what my future would be like. It was a pretty heavy load for a 20-year-old kid to be dealing with. I did the best I could and tried to keep a positive attitude, but it wasn't easy. The whole situation was surreal. I was either thinking about being shot or worrying about who tried to kill me, while at the same time wondering what my future held now that my plans were dashed. Through it all I was dealing with the most incredible pain I had ever experienced.

The pain from the gunshot wound slowly subsided but it never really went away. Every day was a battle. To make myself feel better, I tried to concentrate on my upcoming surgery date on January 20th when the doctors were to put the steel plate in my head. It's not every day that one looks forward to an operation that includes cutting their skull open and inserting a metal plate, but these were desperate times, indeed. Any change would be good at this point.

I knew, or at least I hoped, once the operation was over, I would be on the path to a normal life. Every day I was able to check off another day on the calendar.

Finally, January 20 arrived, and it was time for me to go back to Flushing Hospital for the operation. As I lay on the operating table waiting for the anaesthesia to be administered, the nurses brought in the instruments needed for the procedure. Much to my surprise and dismay, they laid a drill and what looked like a circular saw next to my head. Up to this point I was cool as a cucumber, but the sight of power tools changed that in a hurry. Luckily, the anaesthesia was administered, and I drifted off. My life was in the hands of the medical staff.

The operation was a success. Jokingly, Dr. Negron quipped that the back of my head was now probably the strongest part of my body. I wasn't out of the woods yet. I had to go to his office regularly to get my brain waves checked. After being cooped up for so long, needless to say, I didn't mind. Once a week, my mother and stepfather Gus drove me into Manhattan for the visit. What a great feeling it was, driving through Queens to Manhattan and being outside the confines of a hospital room or my mother's house.

My recuperation was going as well as it could considering the circumstances, and I was itching to get back to normal life, have a beer, and hang out with my friends. Finally, the day came where I was given permission to do all of those things but on a very scaled back schedule. I still had to be careful.

My newfound freedom happened to coincide with a major news announcement from the NYPD's Police Commissioner Michael Codd and New York City Mayor Abraham Beame. On March 10th, 1977, a press conference was held to announce that the NYPD ballistics department had determined that four seemingly random shootings in the Bronx and Queens, including mine, were all connected, and the work of a murderer they dubbed the .44 Caliber killer. Deputy Inspector Timothy Dowd was placed in charge of the Operation Omega task force that was to attempt to solve the case.

I was stunned and also more than a little ecstatic. I was vindicated! These shootings were totally random and had nothing to do with me personally. I had done nothing wrong and I wasn't targeted. Both my mother and the two detectives were wrong, and now everyone knew it.

That euphoric feeling dissipated quickly. It didn't take long before I realized it was a crazed serial killer who shot me. Now I had a whole new set of questions and none of them were good. Why would a serial killer decide to try and kill me? Maybe I was targeted after all. Who was this person? What drove him to kill? Did any of the other victims have something in common with me? As it turned out, I was no closer to an answer about who shot me than I was when the police thought it was a shooting related to a drug deal. Until this person was caught, I wasn't going to be able to rest easy at night.

Two

David Berkowitz was born in Brooklyn, New York, on June 1, 1953. His birth name was Richard Falco, but he was given away to the state by his mother a few days after he came into the world. His birth mother was impoverished, and the rumour was that Berkowtiz was the result of a tryst between her and a married man. His father wanted nothing to do with him.

He was adopted by Pearl and Nathan Berkowitz of the Bronx, who quickly renamed him David. The couple were childless in middle age and owned a hardware store. Berkowitz was chubby as a child and was often teased. He was known as a moody child and a loner who would often pick on children smaller than him.

He wasn't a perfect child by any stretch of the imagination. He was often in trouble and was thought of as difficult. At 12, he began to set fires and killed his mother's parakeet by poisoning it. Apparently, he considered it a rival for his mother's attention. Despite all of this, he never had any serious problems in school or with the legal system.

He joined the United States Army at 17, serving in South Korea and later Fort Knox. After he was discharged honourably, he got a job sorting letters for the post office. While he had stopped setting fires for a while, at the age of 20 he started up again.

Then he started acting really weird.

The official story is that on Christmas Eve, 1975 Berkowitz stabbed two women with a knife. Both survived, but one, Michelle Forman, was hospitalized. He was never suspected of this crime and went on living his apparently normal life. Since the knife attack apparently didn't have the desired outcome for him, he switched to a gun and began his reign of terror in New York City, specifically in the Bronx, Queens, and Brooklyn.

In theory, he sought out women with long hair, although he often attacked more than one victim at once. Many of his attacks, like mine, were geared towards women who were with a man in a parked car. It was said that he would return to the scene of the crime afterwards, to revel in his actions.

The killings had begun the previous summer on a quiet street in the east Bronx. In later chapters, I will go into these shootings much more in depth than I do here. What follows is just a brief summary.

At around one in the morning on the night of July 29, 1976, 18-year-old Donna Lauria and her 19-year old friend, Jody Valenti, were just getting home from a night out at a disco. When Lauria opened the door of the car to get out, she saw a man approaching on foot.

Startled, she began to confront the man, then suddenly he pulled a gun out of a paper bag, crouched down, and shot her. She was killed instantly. The man then shot Valenti in the thigh, then shot once more. The last shot missed both women. The killer then turned and walked away. Valenti survived. Later she told authorities she didn't recognize the killer, but she described him as a white male in his thirties, about 5'9 and with a medium build. She described his hair as short, dark, and curly. Lauria's father told authorities he saw a man matching that description sitting in a yellow car before the shooting.

Rosemary and I were next to be shot.

Then Donna DeMasi, 16, and Joanne Lomino, 18, were both shot and wounded while chatting on a porch in Queens a bit after midnight on the evening of November 27, 1976. A man who they described as being in his 20s approached them and began to ask directions, saying, "Can you tell me how to get…" before he pulled out a gun and fired. He shot numerous times, hitting each of them once. A neighbour told police she saw a blonde man running away from the scene of the crime with a gun in his hand. DeMasi recovered, but Lomino was shot in the back. Sadly, her injuries rendered her a paraplegic.

The shootings continued. On January 30, 1977 at around 12:40 A.M., Christine Freund was shot and killed in Queens; her fiancé John Diel was wounded during the attack. They were sitting in his car after having seen a movie together when numerous shots were fired into the vehicle by an unknown assailant. Diel drove off in a panic, having suffered minor injuries. Freund was not so lucky. She was shot twice and died. Neither saw their attacker.

At around 7:30 P.M. on March 18, 1977, 19-year-old college student Virginia Voskerichian was approached by an armed man while walking home from school. She lifted her books in front of her face in a desperate attempt to protect herself, but to no avail. She was shot through the head and killed.

The city was in a panic.

At 3 A.M. on April 17, 1977, Alexander Esau, 20, and Valentina Suriani, 18, were shot and killed while sitting in a car in the Bronx, just a few blocks away from the Lauria-Valenti shooting. Each was shot twice, neither was able to describe the attacker before they died. Police said the weapon used for the crime was the same one used in earlier shootings.

Police discovered a handwritten letter near the bodies of Esau and Suriani. The letter expressed the killer's determination to continue his work, and taunted police for their fruitless efforts to capture him. The letter also gave the world a name for the killer as he called himself the "Son of Sam".

The New York papers jumped all over this news. This was the biggest story in the city. Every day numerous pages were dedicated to the case, helping to create a city living in fear. Even in the biggest city in the country and during a sweltering summer a lot of people decided to stay indoors to avoid being attacked by the killer. The fear was palpable.

The killer had a type, police said. His targets were mostly young, white, middle-class women who wore their hair long and dark. Many of the victims were brown-haired females, sitting in the passenger seat of a car with a boyfriend. I now thought I understood why I was a target; my assailant had mistaken me for a woman. Women with long, brown hair were flooding the local hair salons, dying their hair blonde or chopping it off short. Females taking a random walk around town, with or without their boyfriends were considered legitimate risk takers. Anxious parents brought their kids in from the streets as soon as the sun went down. The Son of Sam had put into motion a frenzy of fear unparalleled in the history of New York.

The NYPD created a task force to solve the case and assigned close to 300 officers to find the shooter. They checked out the 400 New Yorkers who had permits for .44-caliber revolvers. They investigated current and former mental patients. They consulted with psychics and astrologers. They even watched the TV cop drama, *Starsky and Hutch*, to see if they could gain insight into the killer.

It wasn't just me that was scared now; millions of other people were too.

The mysterious .44 Caliber Killer wrote a second letter to the *New York Daily News* reporter, Jimmy Breslin, three months later. The message was a taunting one, promising more shootings and daring the police to end the mayhem. The letter was signed the SON OF SAM.

On the envelope was printed Blood and Family –
Darkness and Death – Absolute Depravity – .44.

The contents of the letter were:

*Hello from the gutters of N.Y.C. which are filled
with dog manure, vomit, stale wine, urine and
blood. Hello from the sewers of N.Y.C. which
swallow up these delicacies when they are washed
away by the sweeper trucks. Hello from the cracks
in the sidewalks of N.Y.C. and from the ants that
dwell in these cracks and feed in the dried blood
of the dead that has settled into the cracks. J.B.,
I'm just dropping you a line to let you know that
I appreciate your interest in those recent and
horrendous .44 killings. I also want to tell you
that I read your column daily and I find it quite
informative. Tell me Jim, what will you have for
July twenty-ninth? You can forget about me if you
like because I don't care for publicity. However
you must not forget Donna Lauria and you cannot
let the people forget her either. She was a very,
very sweet girl but Sam's a thirsty lad and he won't
let me stop killing until he gets his fill of blood. Mr.
Breslin, sir, don't think that because you haven't
heard from me for a while that I went to sleep.
No, rather, I am still here. Like a spirit roaming
the night. Thirsty, hungry, seldom stopping to rest;
anxious to please Sam. I love my work. Now, the
void has been filled. Perhaps we shall meet face
to face someday or perhaps I will be blown away
by cops with smoking .38's. Whatever, if I shall
be fortunate enough to meet you I will tell you all
about Sam if you like and I will introduce you to
him. His name is "Sam the terrible." Not knowing
what the future holds I shall say farewell and I will
see you at the next job. Or should I say you will*

see my handiwork at the next job? Remember Ms. Lauria. Thank you. In their blood and from the gutter "Sam's creation" .44 Here are some names to help you along. Forward them to the inspector for use by N.C.I.C: "The Duke of Death" "The Wicked King Wicker" "The Twenty Two Disciples of Hell" "John 'Wheaties' – Rapist and Suffocator of Young Girls. PS: Please inform all the detectives working the slaying to remain. P.S: JB, Please inform all the detectives working the case that I wish them the best of luck. "Keep 'em digging, drive on, think positive, get off your butts, knock on coffins, etc." Upon my capture I promise to buy all the guys working the case a new pair of shoes if I can get up the money.

Son of Sam

After picking his jaw off the floor, Breslin notified police and the *New York Daily News* published portions of the letter in an edition that sold over one million copies, their largest sale ever at the time. This caused a whole new flurry of activity, not to mention panic. Police received thousands of tips. Now this lunatic was not only committing serial murder, but he was taunting the police, and in a very bizarre way. Police released a psychological profile of the killer, theorizing he was a neurotic, probably paranoid schizophrenic, and that he believed he was possessed by the devil. Not exactly someone you'd want to hang out with.

While the rest of New York City became more fearful by the day, I felt safer the day the story came out than I had in the last eight months. This guy wasn't after me. He was after everyone. I could finally rest easy. Headlines screamed "NO ONE IS SAFE FROM SON OF SAM".

The attacks continued. On June 26, 1977, Sal Lupo, 20, and Judy Placido, 17, had just left a club in Queens and were sitting in Lupo's parked car. It was 3 in the morning. Out of nowhere, three shots were fired into the vehicle. Lugo was hit in the right arm while Placido was shot in the temple, shoulder, and neck. Both survived. Just moments before they were shot, they were talking about the Son of Sam murders. Neither victim saw who shot them, but two witnesses saw a tall man with dark hair wearing a leisure suit run from the area. One victim said they saw him flee in a car; they even were able to get a partial license plate number.

All was quiet for a month, then on July 31, 1977, Robert Violante and Stacy Moskowitz, both 20, were parked in a car near a park in the Bath Beach neighbourhood. They were making out when a man approached the passenger side of the car. The assailant fired four times, hitting both victims in the head. Moskowitz died, while Violante lost one of his eyes.

On the night of the shooting of Stacy Moskowitz and Robert Violante, Cecilia Davis was walking her dog near the scene of the crime when she saw a police officer put a parking ticket on a nearby car. Moments later she saw a man walk past her who had some sort of "dark object" in his hand. He looked at her in a way that made her uncomfortable. She hurried home only to hear shots fired in the street moments afterwards. A few days later she called the police, who then began to check every car that had been ticketed in the area that evening.

One of the cars that received a ticket was a yellow 1970 Ford Galaxie owned by David Berkowitz. The NYPD called the Yonkers police, asking them to help them track him down, just doing their due diligence. When they did so, the Yonkers police said they had their own issues with Berkowitz. Apparently, he had shot Sam Carr's dog because its barking was keeping him from sleeping. After the dog recovered, Berkowitz claimed that it began speaking to him and demanding that he kill people. Not only that, Berkowitz wrote Carr seemingly demented letters threatening his life and that of his dog.

Berkowitz was also sending bizarre letters to a neighbour of his named Craig Glassman, one reading in part, "How dare you force me into the night to do your bidding . . . True, I am the killer, but, Craig, the killings are your commands . . . The streets have been filled with blood, Glassman, at your request." Needless to say, the NYPD were interested in checking this guy out a little closer.

On August 10, 1977, police went to take a look at Berkowitz's car which was on the street near his apartment building. Amazingly enough, they saw a rifle on the back seat. When they searched the car, they found ammunition, maps of the crime scenes, and a threatening letter addressed to a member of the task force the police set up to catch the Son of Sam. The search of the car was based on the fact there was a rifle visible.

The police waited outside of the apartment as they didn't have a warrant. Later that evening, Berkowitz left his apartment and got in his car, it was at this point that he was arrested.

The NYPD quickly announced that they had arrested David Berkowitz as the lone gunman in the Son of Sam rampage. He had confessed immediately. When the police first encountered him, he said, "You've got me!"

"Who do I have?" one detective asked.

"The Son of Sam," he replied.

It was over. I thought the last piece of the puzzle was answered. It seemed like I could finally relax.

Berkowitz wasn't quite the monster many had been picturing. The killer who had terrified New York City turned out to be a chubby, non-threatening-looking oddball who worked for the post office.

When the police searched his apartment, they were blown away. There was graffiti all over the walls which they considered Satanic in nature, as well as notebooks in which Berkowitz detailed well over 1,000 arsons that he claimed to have committed over the years.

The next day, Berkowitz confessed to the shootings. He said one of the main reasons he killed was that his neighbour's dog told him to, and that it wanted the blood of pretty, young girls. He told the cops that "Sam" was a guy named Sam Carr, who used to be his neighbour. Apparently, the dog was his and was possessed by an ancient demon. A few weeks later, Berkowitz told the press, "There are other Sons out there, God help the world." While most thought this was just the ramblings of a lunatic, many took it as him alluding to having accomplices.

He admitted he made up the whole talking dog story in hopes he would be found not criminally responsible at trial because he was insane. In 1979, Berkowitz said his claims of demonic possession were a hoax and that he had wanted to get even with the world for a long time. According to Berkowitz, the insane writings on the wall and the general disarray of the apartment was a carefully executed plan to make it look like he was a crazed lone gunman.

Despite all of his effort, he was found competent to stand trial. He plead guilty in court and was sentenced to 25-years-to-life in prison for each murder, to be served consecutively.

In July of 1979, while incarcerated in Attica prison, Berkowitz's neck was slashed by another prisoner. He refused to snitch on his attacker, saying it was the punishment he deserved. Many years later, it was revealed by the *New York Post* that the slasher was William Hauser who was incarcerated for first-degree assault at the time. After his release from prison on the assault charges, Hauser wound up being convicted for murder and was given a 25-years to life sentence for savagely beating a man to death with a rolling pin in 1990. While Berkowitz has been said to be a model prisoner, his parole has continually been denied.

While in prison, Berkowitz claimed he was part of a satanic cult, and that he had only killed three of the Son of Sam victims, Donna Lauria, Alexander Esau, and Valentina Suriani. He not only said there were other shooters, but that the cult was involved in planning all of the killings and acting as getaway drivers and lookouts. While he said he couldn't name most of the members of the cult, for fear he would be endangering his family, he did name John and Michael Carr, who are now both deceased. If that last name sounds familiar, it's because they're the sons of Sam Carr, the owner of the talking dog.

I didn't know it at the time, but the arrest and subsequent incarceration of the infamous Son of Sam was just the beginning of my forty-year quest to identify the members of a Satanic cult known as the 22 Disciples of Hell. From 1993 on, I've been investigating and talking to law enforcement, anyone I could, to help me shed light on what happened. I was, and I still am to this day, 100 percent sure other people were involved, and David Berkowitz didn't shoot me.

Three

Maury Terry was a lot of things to a lot of different people.

To some, he was a brilliant investigative reporter, the guy that dedicated his life to make sure the world knew the truth about the Son of Sam murders. To others, he was a successful TV producer and a writer. Some people in his life knew him as a musician and a songwriter. He was a scratch golfer and someone with an encyclopaedic knowledge of Doo-wop. He was smart, witty, a hard drinker, and a heavy smoker. He was always quick with a quip and a great friend to most, but if he wasn't your friend you knew it. Damon Runyan had nothing on him.

As a victim of the Son of Sam attacks and as someone who investigated the case with Maury for years, I had a different viewpoint about Maury than most. To me, he was my friend, my mentor, and my champion. Later on, things became a bit more complicated.

From the very beginning of the Son of Sam shootings, Maury was tireless at attempting to find out who else other than David Berkowitz was involved in the murders, and he kept at it until the day he died. While others were on board with the theory, it was Maury who was front and center at uncovering the vast conspiracy behind the shootings. And he never stopped working at it. He kept the story alive for 44 years and counting. I will always be grateful to Maury and his work.

It wasn't all smooth sailing with Maury. With a personality like his, how could it be? There were a lot of things we didn't agree on, even some involving the Son of Sam case. He could be demanding, controlling, and obstinate. He felt that the investigation around the Son of Sam case was his and his alone to lead and command and because of that, he was duplicitous at times.

The first time I heard of Maury Terry was in 1987 when I read a newspaper review about a new book about the Son of Sam murders called *The Ultimate Evil*. The premise of the book was that David Berkowitz, who was still in prison for being the perpetrator of the murders, didn't act alone. Instead, the book purported he was one of numerous hitmen for a dangerous satanic cult, an offshoot of the Process Church of the Final Judgment. Considering one of the reasons that Berkowitz was in prison was for shooting me in the head, needless to say, this book had my interest. My mind was blown.

This wasn't the first time this theory came to my attention. I initially heard about a conspiracy angle in 1980 during a civil case the victims of Son of Sam, including me, had initiated against Berkowitz. I ended up getting a whopping 2,400 dollars for my near-death experience from that litigation.

Some in the group of victims were represented by Harry Lipsig, a famed New York tort lawyer who over the years had won millions of dollars in damage awards for clients that had been widowed, orphaned, injured, maimed, or otherwise affected by someone being negligent in some way. The guy was such a good talker he could convince a Yankees fan to like the Red Sox.

During the trial, Lipsig kept telling the judge that other people were involved in the shootings. I asked my lawyer what the heck Lipsig was talking about and he explained to me that there was a rumour going around that Berkowitz didn't act alone.

This was news to me. There wasn't the Internet or social media back then so one had to rely on the newspaper for facts. All I had read in the mainstream news was that Berkowitz, the man who supposedly shot me and tried to end my life, was a crazed killer that got his commands to kill from a dog. I was interested in the theory, but I didn't really have anything to go on and I put it in the back of my mind.

The review of *The Ultimate Evil* said the book revealed how author Maury Terry recounted his investigation of the Berkowitz case in intricate detail, including his interviews with the killer from his jail cell, in which Berkowitz confirmed Terry's suspicions about the cult of murder he was involved in. A cult that in theory still has an active underground following to this day. Maury wasn't buying that Berkowitz was a single shooter. He made it his mission to uncover the hidden facts of this case and reveal the true mastermind behind these crimes as well as behind many other ritualistic homicides he attributed to the cult.

I got the book immediately and started reading it on a Friday night. I was planning to read for a short while and then go out and hit the town with some friends. The next thing I knew, a drop of sweat hit the book from my forehead. I looked at the clock on my bedside table and it was 2 A.M. I went to bed, woke up, and finished it first thing in the morning. I read the 600 plus page book in less than two days. My feelings were all over the map. I was stunned, mesmerized, and intrigued.

It all made sense. Well most of it did anyway. When I met Maury, one of the first things I told him was how good the book was, but that he should have ended it earlier and left out the stuff about California and Manson and all that. I felt that it just muddied the waters. Up until that part of the book it was awesome. He didn't like that a whole lot. Maury never was one who handled criticism well.

In Maury's opinion, the police hadn't worked too hard when it came to trying to figure things out once they had

Berkowitz. The case was closed. The public was terrorized by the ".44 Caliber Killer," and subsequently the Son of Sam, and once they busted Berkowitz and he admitted he was the killer, they were done with it. They had someone to blame it on and the killing stopped. To them it was over, and who could blame them really? The pressure was off.

There was never any doubt to me that Berkowitz was involved and was behind a few of the killings and Maury didn't deny that either, but so many things just didn't add up when it came to him being a lone shooter. The fact remains that various composite images of the shooter made by witnesses and surviving victims that are radically different were ignored by the police. The reports of strange people loitering in neighbourhoods shortly before the murders was ignored. The testimony of a woman who saw Berkowitz wandering around and driving around in another area shortly before another shooting he was blamed for was ignored.

And then what about the letters? It was pretty clear to all they weren't written by the same person. Everything about them was different.

In *The Ultimate Evil*, Terry drew a line from Berkowitz to alleged friends of his named the Carrs who allegedly were involved in a cult and were, conveniently enough, murdered shortly after the Son of Sam murders.

Some might write this all off as a conspiracy theory, but Maury made it seem entirely plausible. One thing that he received criticism for is much of the book is speculative and relies on anonymous sources who could have been mistaken or lying, but to be fair, Maury did his best to verify their claims through research.

Maury was able to procure an interview with David Berkowitz in jail in 1993 and segments of the interview appeared on *Inside Edition*. Of course, I had to check it out. As I was watching the show, my ears perked up when I heard my name mentioned. When Maury questioned Berkowitz when it came to the shooting involving me, Berkowitz responded that while he was present at the shooting, he dropped a bombshell that he did not pull the trigger. Even more interesting to me was he claimed he knew who did.

As this line of questioning continued, Maury pressed Berkowitz on who the shooter in my case actually was. Berkowitz responded that it was a woman who shot me, but he would not reveal her name. I couldn't believe it. Was I ever going to be able to put this to rest?

This interview spurred on a new interest in the case by the media and before long I was approached by several television stations to do interviews and to get my take and response around these new allegations. Among those who approached me were producers from the Geraldo Rivera show.

The associate producer of the show knew I worked in Manhattan and asked if I would mind taking the subway up to Kennedy's on 57th street and sharing a limo ride to the Secaucus, NJ studio with another guest, who turned out to be Maury Terry. The only instruction I received from the associate producer was Maury would be at the back bar.

I had never been to Kennedy's, so I had no idea what to expect. I walked in and headed straight to the back bar. It was immediately apparent to me I was out of my league. The place attracted an array of famous people from all walks of life. It was pretty much the place to be seen for a certain crowd. It was filled with lots of famous actors, very high-level law enforcement personnel, and a lot of news people, from TV and radio. The back bar was small, but it fit an unbelievable amount of ego. Everybody was a star in that room.

As soon as I hit the bar, I was immediately greeted by Maurice, one of the best and well-known bartenders in Manhattan. He was the kind of guy that would remember your drink and your name even if you just met him once. He shook my hand, brought me a beer, and introduced me to Maury. We hit it off like we were long-lost brothers. We opted to skip dinner and instead spent our time at the bar with Maurice. That wouldn't be the last time we made that decision.

By the time the limo came to bring us to the studio, a bond had been formed between us. We spent the ride to Jersey talking about the Son of Sam case and Maury's work and theories. This became one of the turning points of my life. I was hooked. While I was once a victim of a crime, from now on I would be an investigator.

To be honest, I don't remember much of the interview with Geraldo, I only spoke briefly. As usual, Maury took center stage, spending much of his time talking about his recently-aired jailhouse interview with David Berkowitz. We rode back to Manhattan together, then we split up, me taking the LIRR home and Maury taking the Metro North to his home in Yonkers.

As we hit it off and had an obvious mutual interest, we decided to stay in touch but the only way to communicate with Maury was through his landline telephone. He was old school in every way. He had no cell phone, no email, not even a beeper. Later on, I found out that he didn't even have a PC at home.

For the next five years, we talked on the phone numerous times a week. We always had a good time talking, but the only problem with the phone calls were how long they lasted. Sometimes our calls would go on for hours on end; at the very least, they would be an hour long. My wife. and later my daughter, used to kid me about being on the phone with "my girlfriend Maury."

Maury could be touchy. If I missed one of his calls, Maury would get pissed off if I didn't call him back immediately. I knew I needed to set aside a big block of time to talk to him which wasn't always easy. Sometimes three or four days would go by until I had enough time to call him back. When that happened, he would rip into me as soon as

I picked up the phone about how long it took me to get back to him. Like I said, Maury had ego.

We kept meeting pretty much once a month at Kennedy's until the bar closed in 2011. For much of this time, it was my entire social life. I used to be pretty active in the bar scene when I was younger, but at this point in my life I was raising my daughter Casey alone and didn't have much free time to go out. My life was work, taking care of Casey, and, once a month, hanging with Maury and the folks at Kennedy's. It was a time of my life that was very structured.

At first, I was a little uncomfortable rubbing shoulders with all the news personalities, movie and television stars, and high-ranking law enforcement that frequented Kennedy's. I was more used to dive bars than this type of place. My first couple of visits I listened and smiled and nodded my head a lot. What do I talk about to news anchors like David Diaz or famous actors like Jerry Orbach? I was just a regular guy. Maury always made sure he introduced me to everybody he knew, and if he didn't know the person very well, he would nod at Maurice and in a minute, he would introduce me to the person in question. Eventually, I felt at home in Kennedy's and developed several solid friendships.

Cliff Gorman, the actor and Tony award winner known for his portrayal of Lenny Bruce on Broadway, lived across the street from Kennedy's and was very good friends with Maury. Usually Cliff didn't come into the bar until 11:00 P.M. or so. By that time, a lot of the customers had left, and it was just the regulars that were still hanging out. Cliff would regale us with stories from the movies or plays he was a part of, but what really bonded the two of them was their love of Doo Wop.

One night, about 2:00 in the morning, the three of us left Kennedy's to go home. Maury was heading to Yonkers, I was going to Floral Park, and Cliff was just walking across the street. Maury started singing the opening bass line of the Devotions' "Rip Van Winkle" … Ba Bom-Ba Bom-ba-

ba bom-bom-bom. Cliff picked up the harmony with Maury singing the silly words of the song and I continued to deliver that bass line. It was a simple time in life, but one I treasure to this day. I miss both of those guys.

I always looked forward to our meetings at Kennedy's. The company was good, and the talk eventually turned to the Son of Sam case. Besides talking to Maury on the phone, I didn't have anyone else to talk to about what was really going on with the case, which was still a huge part of my life. Most of my circle of friends were sold on the NYPD's version of the lone gunman and if I started talking about what I believed, they looked at me like I was nuts. Kennedy's afforded me the opportunity to meet newsmen and law enforcement that shared my belief that more than David Berkowitz was involved in the shootings. We weren't just having fun; we were trying to solve a crime.

Maury not only didn't have a computer, he knew absolutely nothing about the Internet. As time went on, he began to give me information such as a name or an address and I would do the legwork, do some research, and tell him what I found out. He usually wouldn't tell me why he wanted the information, just that he needed it and that it was important. It could be as simple as him giving me an address and me trying to find out information that corresponded with it. Who owned the house, who they bought it from, how long they had owned it, that kind of thing. It wasn't like Maury to give me, or anyone else for that matter, more information than they needed. I found this out the hard way over the years.

Eventually I became pretty proficient at doing this investigative work. Maury finally got a computer after a few years, so we spent a lot of time exchanging documents and photos, but I still kept doing research for him. After a while it got to the point that I was doing my own investigating as well. As each year went by, I became more confident that we were going to find out who shot me. It was just a matter of time.

Four

On April 17th, 1977, the individual who had become known as the .44 Caliber Killer shot and killed Alexander Esau and Valentina Suriani on the Hutchinson River Parkway Service Road in the Pelham Bay section of the Bronx.

As the NYPD cordoned off the crime scene, a four-page note left by the killer was found. The letter was addressed to Captain Borelli of the NYPD.

The letter was printed in capitalized, slanted block letters. It said:

DEAR CAPTAIN JOSEPH BORELLI,

I AM DEEPLY HURT BY YOUR CALLING ME A WEMON HATER. I AM NOT.

BUT I AM A MONSTER.

I AM THE "SON OF SAM." I AM A LITTLE "BRAT."

WHEN FATHER SAM GETS DRUNK HE GETS MEAN. HE BEATS HIS FAMILY. SOMETIMES HE TIES ME UP To THE BACK OF THE HOUSE. OTHER TIMES HE LOCKS ME IN THE GARAGE. SAM LOVES TO DRINK BloOD.

"GO OUT AND KILL" COMMANDS FATHER SAM,

BEHIND OUR HOUSE SOME REST. MOSTLY YOUNG – RAPED AND SLAUGHTERED – THIER BLOOD DRAINED – JUST BONES NOW

PAPA SAM KEEPS ME LOCKED IN THE ATTIC, TOO. I CAN'T GET OUT BUT I LOOK OUT THE ATTIC WINDOW AND WATCH THE WORLD GO BY.

I FEEL LIKE AN OUTSIDER. I AM ON A DIFFERENT WAVE LENGTH THEN EVERYBODY ELSE – PROGRAMMED TOO KILL.

HOWEVER, TO STOP ME YOU MUST KILL ME. ATTENTION ALL POLICE: SHOOT ME FIRST – SHOOT TO KILL OR ELSE. KEEP OUT OF MY WAY OR YOU WILL DIE!

PAPA SAM IS OLD NOW. HE NEEDS SOME BLOOD TO PRESERVE HIS YOUTH. HE HAS HAD TOO MANY HEART ATTACKS. TOO MANY HEART ATTACKS. "UGH, ME HOOT IT URTS SONNY BOY."

I MISS MY PRETTY PRINCESS MOST OF ALL. SHE'S RESTING IN OUR LADIES HOUSE BUT I'LL SEE HER SOON.

I AM THE "MONSTER" – "BEELZEBUB" – THE "CHUBBY BEHEMOUTH."

I LOVE TO HUNT. PROWLING THE STREETS LOOKING FOR FAIR GAME – TASTY MEAT. THE WEMON OF QUEENS ARE Z PRETTYIST OF ALL. I MUST BE THE WATER THEY DRINK. I LIVE FOR THE HUNT – MY LIFE. BLOOD FOR PAPA.

MR. BORELLI, SIR, I DONT WANT TO KILL ANYMORE NO SIR, NO MORE BUT I MUST, "HONOUR THY FATHER."

I WANT TO MAKE LOVE TO THE WORLD. I LOVE PEOPLE. I DON'T BELONG ON EARTH. RETURN ME TO YAHOOS.

TO THE PEOPLE OF QUEENS, I LOVE YOU. AND I WA WANT TO WISH ALL OF YOU A HAPPY EASTER. MAY GOD BLESS YOU IN THIS LIFE AND IN THE NEXT AND FOR NOW I SAY GOODBYE AND GOODNIGHT.

POLICE- LET ME HAUNT YOU WITH THESE WORDS;

I'LL BE BACK!

I'LL BE BACK!

TO BE INTERRPRETED AS – BANG BANG, BANG, BANG, BANG – UGH!!

YOURS IN MURDER

MR. MONSTER

Strangely, the Borelli letter was not released in full to the media or the public for over four months. Even the rank-and-file members of the .44 Caliber Killer task force were not privy to the contents of the letter. But both the *NY Post* and *NY Daily News*, using their sources within the NYPD, knew at least some of its content. Maury always asserted withholding the letter was a significant error by the NYPD. The clues that were contained in this missive, if used correctly, might have led to an arrest months sooner, saving lives in the process.

The NYPD brass used the clues in the letter to attempt to build a profile of the killer. The line "Too many heart attacks. Ugh, me hoot it urts sonny boy" was deciphered by the police as words meant to be heard in a Scottish accent. But what did that mean? Was the killer Scottish? If so, it was kind of unlikely he would use such language as it was such an obvious clue, unless he wanted to be caught. They also believed that the mention of heart attacks might be a reference to the killer's father. Or maybe the suspect was mistreated at one point by brown haired nurses? The fact that Donna Lauria was a medical technician and Jody Valente a student nurse fueled this theory. Ironically, the police never explained how the killer would know what the victim's profession was considering the shootings were supposed to be random. The letter also contained many other clues, mentioning a dog, a yard, an attic, and an old man named Sam who drank and was prone to violence.

The people of Queens were mentioned in the letter and the killer wished a Happy Easter to all as well. The letter ends with a taunting threat "I'll be back!", " I'll be back!", " I'll be back!"

Maury pointed out that these statements indicated that the attack alluded to in the letter was to be carried out in Queens a week earlier, around Easter. But the Borelli Letter was left at the Esau-Surriani shooting in the Bronx a week after Easter had come and gone.

Sometime after the Son of Sam shooter dropped the letter at the Esau/Surriani attack, I received a call from a *National Enquirer* reporter requesting an interview. Not thinking about the implications of this, I haphazardly accepted the request and gave the reporter my address. Back then, just as it is now, the *National Enquirer* was not regarded as a legitimate newspaper but more of an exploitive tabloid. The caller had a strange accent that in retrospect I thought might be Scottish. When I told my mother about the pending interview and my thoughts about the guy's accent, she recommended that I contact the police. I called the 109Th Precinct where the Omega task force was headquartered and told a detective about the interview request from a reporter with a Scottish accent. As previously stated, the Borelli letter had a few lines that led the NYPD to think the writer was "talking" in a Scottish accent (Ugh, me hoot it urts sonny boy.")

They told me to go ahead with the interview and they would set up surveillance. The morning of the interview about 15 detectives showed up at my mother's house. They parked an unmarked van in front of the house, manned by four armed cops. Four or five cops were stationed around the perimeter of our house and three cops were on the second floor of the house. The last person on the team was a detective standing behind the front door right next to me. As the reporter walked up the walkway and knocked on the door, I opened the door to greet him and the detectives pounced on him. No shots were fired, and the reporter was taken down and handcuffed. As it turned out, the reporter was legitimate, really worked for the *National Enquirer*, and had an Australian accent. I guess I am not an expert on accents.

Needless to say, the cuffs were removed, apologies given and accepted, and the interview never happened. I wish I could remember the name of the reporter. If you're reading this now, I would like to apologize to you for putting you through that.

The letter to Jimmy Breslin was mailed on May 30th, 1977. It was dropped in a mailbox by an unknown person in Englewood, New Jersey. When Breslin opened the letter, he must have been shocked to see that he had just received a missive from none other than the Son of Sam. The letter was handwritten and loaded with clues, but it was apparent to any discerning reader that the style of this letter and the previous one was very different.

It was unclear whether the killer was writing letters to well-known people like Breslin because he wanted to be caught or was just enjoying messing with people. Breslin and the *NY Daily News* milked this letter for a few days by teasing the public with the fact that it existed before it was printed in the paper, thus building up the tension in the city and ensuring maximum exposure. Once the paper released the entire letter, it set off a frenzy unlike any that New

York had ever seen. Everyone in the city became sleuths overnight and was trying to solve the case. It was difficult to go anywhere in the city without hearing people talk about it.

If one looked at the two letters from the killer, they didn't seem to be from the same person. Unlike the letter left at the Bronx shooting, the Breslin letter was written by what seemed to be a creative and talented writer. The first letter was composed of short choppy phrases while the Breslin letter was very well thought out, with perfect punctuation and very descriptive. Jimmy Breslin even commented about the quality of the writing. It was difficult to imagine that the same individual crafted both of these communications.

The letter to Breslin contained additional clues regarding the killings including a reference to three other potential suspects and something called "The Twenty-Two Disciples of Hell." One of the three people named was "John Wheaties"—Rapist and suffocater of Young Girls." Okay, sure he didn't sound like a very cool guy to say the least. But what was this to mean? Interestingly enough "John Wheaties" was listed in the Yonkers phone book. Sam Carr gave this moniker to his son, John, and his daughter, Wheat, for one of the many telephone lines that belonged to the Carr Answering Service. John and Wheat had shared the line since they were teenagers.

Besides the names that in theory were "to help the police along" the writer urges Breslin to "Forward them to the Inspector for use by N.C.I.C". This is in reference to the National Crime Information Center. Back in 1977, most of the general public had little to no clue what the N.C.I.C was. This led the police to think the killer had a law enforcement background.

In the second P.S. of the letter, the writer wishes the detectives working on the case good luck and proceeds with "Keep 'em digging, drive on, think positive, get off your butts, knock on coffins, etc.".

Maury always was a sucker for a good riddle. He eventually concluded that these were in fact physical directions to the home of Berkowitz.

In his mind, "Keep 'em digging" became Peek, meaning "Look" "em "became "me" and "digging" was shortened to "Digs", which is a slang word for home.

In other words, Look for me home.

Then he took "drive on" and figured "drive" could be another name for a street or an avenue, then "on" could be reversed to "no", which could mean drive north.

When it came to "think positive", Maury assumed the clue was" think" could be "head" and "positive" could be "right".

In other words, he thought in reality it was "head right."

When it came to "get off your butts" it was a bit tricky, but he thought "butt" could be a cigarette ash.

GET OFF ASH

When it came to "knock on coffins", he figured that coffins were made from pine so to Maury it became "knock on Pine."

It appeared, at least to Maury, the letter was directions to Berkowitz's apartment on Pine Street.

When I first read *The Ultimate Evil,* I found Maury's explanation for this part of the letter fascinating. It was amazing to me he could come up with something like this. In the ensuing years, as I became more immersed in the investigation, my view of that passage being directions to David Berkowitz's has changed a bit. You have to admit Maury's translation is a bit of a leap. I do not know what the real meaning of that passage is, but it is hard for me to believe the writer was giving directions to his house. I'll let you be the judge.

The letter was signed "Son of Sam" and there were strange graphics scrawled below the name. The police mistakenly thought it may have been a universal sign for man and woman. They were wrong. The symbol had its origins with Elephas Levi, an 18th century occultist. The "signs" were actually the astrological signs for Mars, the god of war, and Venus, goddess of the Roman Sewers, who was also known as Placida.

As previously noted, the Breslin Letter was mailed on May 30, 1977 and contained the strange graphic below Son of Sam's name. Although the 7th attack was still a month away, it seems the writer referenced through the graphic some clues to the future attack at the Elephas disco in Bayside. Besides the obvious connection to Elephas Levi's name, one of the surviving victims, Judy Placido's name is very similar to the goddess of Roman sewers, Placida. In my opinion, that is quite a coincidence.

This was all the kind of thinking that made a hero out of Maury to many, and a laughingstock to others. The whole Pine Street thing didn't just go away, though. In the later days, when Maury's small inner circle of researchers started to investigate the case, he called us "the Pine Street Irregulars."

Five

Although outwardly Maury played it off like he was a tough investigator who didn't let anything rattle him, on the inside he was extremely nervous about possible retribution from some of these people that we were investigating. While his book was published in 1987, Maury was concerned years before that about being messed with by members of the cult because the word was out that he was trying to dig up information about the killings. He was pretty paranoid about it and tried to keep things below ground. After all, he knew better than anyone what these people were capable of. He had an unlisted number and he often used fake names to identify himself while traveling. When *The Ultimate Evil* came out he even included this passage to help ensure his safety, "If my safety or that of anyone close to me is ever jeopardized, several people whose names grace the top of a special list will come under rapid and intense scrutiny."

It wasn't just his physical safety he was concerned about, he was also worried about lawsuits. Wheat Carr, a police dispatcher in Yonkers, whose father, Sam Carr, was said to be the "Sam" in question that Berkowitz was fixated on, had threatened to sue Maury more than once.

The Process Church was another one of his worries. Maury pointed his finger at the Process Church of the Final Judgment as being at the heart of the murderous conspiracy. A church that, in theory, worships Jesus and Satan equally, was tied to Charles Manson, and has a symbol that looks more than a tad like a swastika is bound to get a little attention, even if they weren't looking for it. And they certainly received that attention from Maury.

The Process Church of the Final Judgment was founded in the United Kingdom in 1966 by the British couple, Mary Ann MacLean and Robert de Grimston. They met when they were members of the Church of Scientology. Scientology has its own detractors, of course, but that is a story for another day.

After they left the realm of Scientology, they were married and started a splinter group which eventually morphed into the Process Church. Its members originally lived in a commune in England, then moved to Mexico. They eventually settled in San Francisco where the group began to hit the streets, dressed in black robes, trying to spread their mission.

Maury wasn't the first person to cast aspersions on the Process Church. Prosecutors investigating the Manson murders suggested that there were links between those killings and the Process Church. Although no proof of such a connection was ever found, the allegations damaged the Church's reputation. There were also rumours of them being involved in ritual murders as well as some including animal sacrifice.

Vincent Bugliosi, the prosecutor at the Charles Manson trial, suggested in his book *Helter Skelter,* that Manson may have borrowed philosophically from the Process Church. In his 1972 book, *The Family,* Ed Sanders took it even farther alleging that Manson had once been a member of the Process Church.

The Church sued Sanders. The lawsuit forced him and his publisher to remove the allegation from the book. Terry was afraid they might sue him next. He talked about it to me often. But the lawsuit never came.

The author and Feral House publisher, Adam Parfrey, once said of the Process Church. "One could make the argument that due to its extreme views and insular arrogance, The Process Church had itself to blame for the smears and resulting hysteria. But the fallout of this failed suit loomed large in the cult's toning down of its public face and clamming up in public dialogue about its history."

While the Process has faded from public eye over the years and is rarely mentioned, it still exists in a way. It has transformed into Best Friends Animal Society, an animal welfare organization which exists to this day.

At the time, Maury claimed that the Process Church was a part of a larger Satanic network. He believed that Berkowitz became involved with the cult and Satanism, not because he was insane, but because he was lonely.

I didn't have the same sort of fears as Maury. I was operating behind the scenes; no one really knew I was talking to Maury or spending a lot of time investigating the case, so I wasn't all that worried about retribution, financial or otherwise. Not only that, but it's not like I am swimming in money, a lawsuit against me would not yield a whole lot of profit.

Who knows, maybe I should worry a bit more about retribution at the present time. I am much more up-front with my involvement now and this book will make me even more so, but a lot of these people mentioned are so old at this point, what are they going to do? Are they actually going to get in their car, find me, and shoot me? I doubt it. They would be far more likely to declare their innocence than do that. But I guess I'll find out.

One of the people that I know is involved for certain is a registered sex offender who has a history of molesting children who lives in South Carolina. I know some people working on the case have contacted him in the past, but he just plays dumb. He never pulled the trigger, but he was involved in the murders in a major way. With his age, background, and criminal history, it is much more likely he would fight to prove his innocence before he would try to sue me or kill me.

In my opinion, Maury's biggest fault was that he felt he owned the Son of Sam case, and he and only he, was going to be the one to solve the case and reap the rewards that came with it. Maury was not very open to other people's opinions, including mine; he had too big of an ego. One time I mentioned some information that another true crime writer wrote about the case and he quickly dismissed it out of hand. It was a very minor point, and didn't really mean much to the case, but it really illustrated to me his need to be in control and be the sole authority on the Son of Sam attacks.

For the twenty-something years I knew Maury, most of it was spent discussing and working on the Son of Sam case, but there were several occasions we branched out to other high-profile cases. We did extensive work together after the 911 attacks, honing in on people of interest whose stories did not add up. A few months after the 911 attacks, the anthrax scare presented itself to Maury as another possible case to work on. Letters laced with anthrax began appearing in the U.S. mail and five Americans were killed in what became the worst biological attack in U.S. history. We delved into it and came up with some viable suspects. Unfortunately, Maury didn't share the information that we put together with anyone. As far as I know, nothing ever came of our research.

Maury's theory on the cult, which he considered responsible for the shootings, is clearly laid out in *The Ultimate Evil*. It truly was his life's work. A lot of people don't realize how much time he spent on this even before the book came out. Maury spent eleven years researching the Son of Sam case before the book was published. At some point during this investigation, he met with Jim Rothstein, an NYPD detective whose beat was New York City's infamous 42nd Street. Much of Rothstein's work involved investigating the trafficking of young boys and girls. Detective Rothstein was told by one of his 42nd Street informants that pimps were supplying some well-heeled men of Yonkers with young boys for sex and that Untermeyer Park was the meet up site for this nefarious activity. While investigating this, Detective Rothstein's discovered that a group of satanic worshippers also used the park for their rituals.

In addition to the Satanic rituals and human trafficking in Untermeyer Park, the local teenagers also used the park for keg parties, smoking joints, and whatever else they couldn't do without getting arrested in public. Local residents say that back in the 1970's there could be up to 200 people hanging out in the park on any given night during the summer.

The park was named for Samuel Untermeyer, who was a respected American lawyer and civic leader whose passion was horticulture. He was known for building a 150-acre riverside estate called Greystone, in Yonkers, New York, on the riverbanks of the Hudson. The estate was known for its gardens, which were considered some of the most beautiful in the world at the time.

In order to complete his vision of his gardens, Untermeyer sought help from an expert, so he hired a prominent landscape architect, William Welles Bosworth, in 1906. Ten years later, the estate was gorgeous. It contained numerous gardens with fantastic stonework, many steps, and elaborate terraces. After Untermeyer died in 1940, his property was opened as a public park, owned by the City of Yonkers, but due to the costly maintenance and lack of attention it fell into decay.

By the 1970s, the Yonkers park was all but abandoned. At night, it could be dangerous, inhabited by vagrants and criminals. By that time, the U.S. was in a middle of a Satanic/occult craze that caused panic among some segments of the population as rumours of devil-worshiping cults spread throughout the nation. How much of it was based in fact was difficult to determine. Either way, Untermeyer Park was allegedly used by a kind of Satanic cult that performed mystical rites there, perhaps even involving blood sacrifice.

Even though it has never been officially confirmed, the cult that held its séances in Untermeyer Park was believed to be an offshoot of the notorious Process Church of the Final Judgment, which as stated previously, also purportedly had ties to the Manson Family. Graffiti with upside down crosses and other invocations of Satanic symbolism were found spray-painted on the water pump house of the park, which was nicknamed the Devil's Hole. Overnight workers at a nearby hospital reported seeing torches moving and glowing in the night, accompanied by strange and sinister chanting.

Rumours started circulating in the late 1970s among Yonkers kids of hearing animals crying out in pain within the park. Around the same time, several beheaded and mutilated German Shepherds were found in the aqueducts of the park. Members of the Process had been known to keep German Shepherds as pets.

Maury was convinced there was a connection between the satanic cult involving child trafficking, drugs, and murder, and the Son of Sam case. His findings were later corroborated by his jail house interviews with David Berkowitz in 1993. Maury knew there had to be some sort of a hierarchy within this satanic cult and one of his main goals was finding out who was at the top of it. As we all know, bad people tend to hang out with bad people, but if you cut off the head of the snake, sometimes the whole thing dies.

As in most groups of this nature, the lowest level of the cult was used to carry out the upper level's wishes. In Maury's view, many prominent businessmen and public figures were the recipients of the human trafficking, the purpose of which was sexual. Other members of the cult were involved in drug smuggling and pornography. It's unclear to me how this cult and their known activities were tied to the Son of Sam shootings. Maury Terry contended that the shootings were deliberate hits meant to be initiation into the cult, and not random shootings.

Although I think Maury Terry connected a lot of the dots in this complicated case, I never understood why shooting young New Yorkers were part of the cult's plan other than the aforementioned initiation theory. It is something that Berkowitz has never talked about, nor something Maury had ever legitimately figured out.

Through his research, Maury was able to tie numerous people to the cult's activity. After Berkowitz was arrested, ten people who were thought by Maury to be part of the cult died a violent death within 24 months of Berkowitz' capture including John and Michael Carr. Some of the suspects that Maury was investigating were also being looked at by the Yonkers Police Dept. and the NYPD. Maury's investigation, prior to his book being published, led the Queens District Attorney, John Santucci, to reopen the case, stating that the information his office received warranted further investigation. Nothing ever came of this.

Officially, the NYPD has never wavered from their original assessment that David Berkowitz was the lone shooter in the Son of Sam attacks. But off the record, I have met and talked with over 30 law enforcement officials that believe other people were involved.

The NYPD had no idea whatsoever any of these shootings were related until March of 1977, after the 5th attack. The Son of Sam shooting spree was one of the most complicated cases that most of these law enforcement officers ever worked on and remain so to this day. There was so much conflicting information that even the articles written the day after the shootings often said entirely different things regarding details of the crime.

This case is incredibly complicated to begin with, but it has been made far more so by officials ignoring the evidence in their possession, David Berkowitz changing his story several times, and the fact he pleaded guilty to six murders without going through a trial. Of course, a trial would have produced witnesses that quite probably would have proved that David Berkowitz didn't act alone. To make matters worse, because so many of the unanswered questions went unresolved, they were left for the internet's armchair sleuths to come up with their own theories, which caused even more false information to be out there. In my opinion, all of the misinformation, confusion, and lies about the case could have been averted with a well-thought-out investigation by the authorities.

I helped Maury investigate the case with the goal of updating *The Ultimate Evil*. When new evidence was out there because of the updated book, hopefully the police would ultimately re-open the case. This would allow me to file a lawsuit against the various government agencies affiliated with the investigation, such as the NYPD, Queens DA office, Brooklyn DA office, and Yonkers PD. The optimum scenario would have the case reopened, police and DA records and files would be available, and finally a possible financial gain for myself to compensate me for my injuries and PTSD. I figured the worst that could happen was I would get the case back in the public eye and the press would detail the evidence that was ignored and mishandled by law enforcement back in the 1979-1981 time period. Unfortunately, Maury died before any of this could happen.

Six

As a victim of the Son of Sam killings, I started following the case with great interest once the NYPD revealed that a serial killer was responsible for all of the supposedly random shootings. Prior to that, I, along with 20 million other people, read articles in the newspapers regarding seemingly random shootings without a thought of them being related.

What follows is a summation of the official NYPD view of the Son of Sam shootings as reported by the police and the press a day or two after each attack. In subsequent chapters, I will detail what has been found out about these attacks by law enforcement, as well as by Maury and myself. Some of this information may seem repetitive, but the official story and what really happened are so different that so-called facts of the crime really need to be told as two entirely separate versions.

The Son of Sam shootings began with an attack on victims Donna Lauria and Jody Valenti. The shooting occurred on July 29, 1976 in front of Donna's apartment building: 2860 Buhre Ave. in the Pelham Bay section of the Bronx at approximately 1 A.M.

According to an article in the next day's *Daily News*, the shooter fired four shots into the car the two were in, killing Donna and wounding her friend, Jody Valenti. Apparently, the first bullet, which was fired at close range, crashed through the window on the passenger side and struck Donna in the temple. The second bullet entered the thigh of the driver, Jody Valenti. The third slug ricocheted off the door and the fourth shot was found lodged in the front seat.

Detectives said they believed the murder weapon was a .45 caliber automatic but were not able to confirm this until they received ballistics reports. Donna Lauria's uncle, a police officer who asked not to be publicly identified, said that on the evening in question she had gone with her friend to a Manhattan disco in Jody Valenti's mother's car, a 1975 Oldsmobile Cutlass. He said the girls returned to Ms. Lauria's apartment house about 12:30 A.M., and sat in the car, talking for a few minutes about the events of the night. A short while later, Donna's parents drove up, saw the girls, and chatted with them for a few minutes. Mr. Lauria went to get the family dog so that he and Donna could walk the dog together after Jody left. While he was upstairs in their 4th floor apartment, the gunman snuck up on the girls and shot them.

After the attack, Jody Valenti got out of the car, went around to the other side, and opened the door causing Lauria's body to tumble out and slump onto the pavement. It was at this time that Donna's father came out of the apartment house with the dog. He burst into tears when he saw his daughter's body on the ground. Valenti, a nurse who lived a few blocks away, told detectives she did not recognize the killer, but said he was a white man in his late 30s who wore a blue striped shirt. Donna Lauria had been employed as an emergency medical technician for two years at the Empire State Ambulance Service which had its headquarters at New York Hospital.

In a televised press conference that aired months after the shooting, the NYPD stated that Jody Valenti told them the gun had a long barrel. Commissioner Codd likened the gun to a wild west .44 caliber pistol.

The second attack happened on October 23, 1976 in the North Flushing section of Queens at around 2 A.M. Rosemary Keenan and I had left Pecks Depot Grill and parked Rosemary's car on 159th Street and 33rd Avenue. Minutes after we parked, shots rang out and shattered the windows in her blue Volkswagen Beetle. Rosemary was uninjured by the bullets but sustained cuts from the flying auto glass. I was hit by a bullet fragment in the back of my head. After the shooting, Rosemary drove back to Peck's Bar and Grill, where my friends realized I was bleeding from a head wound and needed medical attention. My friends brought me to Flushing Hospital Emergency Room. In the late morning hours, NYPD homicide detective Marlin Hopkins responded to the shooting report and once Det. Hopkins was assured I would survive my wounds, he left the hospital without any further investigation. Because Rosemary and I both survived the shooting, the incident went unreported to the public.

The third attack occurred on November 27, 1976 at 12:40 A.M. in front of Joanne Lomino's house at 83-31 262 Street in Floral Park Queens. Joanne Lomino and Donna DeMasi had just returned home, first by subway and then via bus, from watching a movie in Manhattan. An Omega Task Force detective, Marlin Hopkins, yes, the same one who came to see me in the hospital, told me years later that the girls got off the bus by the Burger King that was about 5 blocks from Joanne Lomino's house. This differs from the official report that stated the girls got off the bus at 263rd Street, a block from Joanne's house. He also told me that different Burger Kings were a common thread at some of the Son of Sam attacks. Unfortunately, he would not elaborate on that. This fact to the best of my knowledge was never publicly reported by the NYPD.

They were standing on Lomino's stoop talking when a man approached them asking for directions. Before they knew what was happening, he drew a gun from under his coat and fired several shots at the girls. One bullet lodged in Joanne's spine, paralyzing her from the waist down. Donna DeMasi was shot once in the neck, wounding her. DeMasi described the assailant as a white male, between 25 and 30 years old, and wearing a green or brown three-quarter-length coat. According to the November 28, 1976 edition of the *New York Times*, the police found three shell casings at the scene.

The fourth attack occurred on January 30, 1977 at the Long Island Railroad station in Forest Hills, Queens, NY at about 12:40 A.M. Christine Freund and John Diel had gone to see a Rocky movie and grabbed a bite to eat at the Wine Gallery Restaurant. When they left the restaurant, they walked to Diel's car which was parked in the Tudor-style courtyard of the Forest Hills Long Island Railroad station. When they got to the car, Diel started the engine. While the car was warming up, they kissed each other for a few moments. About two minutes later, shots were fired into the car through the unopened windows. Diel said, "the window came in. It didn't sound like a firecracker. It was a bang. Chris slumped over onto my shoulder. Then I ran out of the car and yelled for help." Diel stopped a car at a red light at the intersection of Burns Street and 71st Avenue and hysterically told the couple in the car what happened. They drove him back to his car, left him there, and went to call police. When police arrived, they took the bleeding woman to St. John's Queens Hospital in Elmhurst, Queens, where she died at 4:30 A.M. In a *New York Times* article dated January 31, 1997, Diel told the police he was at first unable to get help, but the police said the people who heard him shout notified the police. Mr. Diel meanwhile went to a nearby intersection at 71st Avenue and Burns Street where he blocked traffic to get the assistance he needed. To further complicate the events, Diel's name is spelled Diel in the *New York Times* and Diehl in the *New York Daily News*.

In a surprise twist to the case, Queens DA John Santucci stated, an effort to "crack this case as quickly possible has been started. We are checking into the possibility that cases with similar circumstances may have occurred in this borough and other boroughs over the past year or so and whether there are any connections between those possible similar cases and this one." Neither Mr. Santucci nor the police cited any specific cases or reasons they thought some of these attacks were related. To the best of my recollection, this is the first time a law enforcement official or a district attorney's office connected the four seemingly random shootings in the Bronx and Queens together.

The fifth shooting victim was Virginia Voskerichian. On March 8, 1977, Virginia, a 19-year-old Columbia University student was shot at point blank range. She died on the scene. She was on her way home from school when people nearby heard screams followed by a shot. The shooting happened less than a hundred yards from where Christine Freund was shot a month earlier. Virginia, who lived with her parents, had just gotten off the subway at Continental Ave and 108th Street in Forest Hills. About two blocks from the subway station, she entered the boundaries of the privately owned Forest Hills Gardens Community, a neighbourhood of Tudor style residences. She was carrying her schoolbooks and a purse, which was found unopened and undisturbed beside her. Virginia was found lying face down on the sidewalk in front of 4 Dartmouth Street, across from the Forest Hills Inn. Officers said that witnesses had seen a young, white man, about 18 years old and about 5 ft 9 inches tall wearing dark clothes, a ski hat, and a waist-length jacket running west on Dartmouth Street immediately after the shooting.

A *New York Times* article printed two days after the shooting said the police were seeking a youth 16 to18 years old in relation to the crime. A man in the quiet and affluent neighbourhood told police he had seen a youth he described as "pudgy" running from the vicinity of the killing. He said the young man had pulled a stocking cap low over his face and muttered "Oh Jesus!" when he passed the witness. The police said they had no evidence to connect Virginia's shooting with the murder of Christine Freund. However, residents of the area, particularly women, were convinced that both women were killed by the same maniac. It was surmised that the killer had a penchant for killing young women. The killings were within a half block of each other and there was no apparent motive for either. The police stated that she had not been sexually molested and that $35 had been found in her purse leaving out robbery as a reason for the killing.

Virginia had transferred to Columbia University from Queens College after her sophomore year because Columbia had a good reputation for Russian courses. She was an A student with a particular proclivity in Russian literature.

According to the police reconstruction of the killing, Virginia left college late in the afternoon either because she had a late class or because she was studying in the library. NYPD believed she left the subway at the Continental Ave. station and walked a few blocks along the brightly-lit and heavily-travelled road. However, when she turned right on Dartmouth street at about 7:30 P.M., there was very little light as the lampposts in that area were designed similar to the ones used in the gaslight era, meaning they had weak bulbs. On this block, one of the bulbs was shattered so that this section was almost entirely unlit. I don't know if this was by design or a coincidence. The police never elaborated on this fact.

On March 10th, the killings were officially publicly tied together by law enforcement. Mayor Abe Beame and NYPD Commissioner Michael Codd spoke at a packed press conference and announced to the public that five seemingly random shootings over the last 9 months were all tied to a .44 caliber gun. Ballistics were not able to determine what type of gun was used in the 5 shootings but had conclusive proof that .44 caliber bullets were used in all attacks. Commissioner Codd also stated that the gun was a western-style revolver. There was little doubt the same person, or persons, was committing these crimes. The next day, the press dubbed the serial killer "The .44 Caliber Killer" sending the city into a panic.

The sixth shooting occurred on April 17, 1977. Alexander Esau, who was 20 years old and a tow truck operator, and Valentina Suriani, 18 years old, a Lehman College student were shot at 3 A.M. on the service road of the Hutchinson River Parkway about a block away from Suriani's home. The couple were long-time friends. They started their evening out together around 9 when they took in a movie together. At the time of the shooting, they were sitting in the front seat of a car. Valentina was behind the driver's wheel when the shots were fired on the driver's side. The car was owned by Esau's brother. A resident of a nearby building heard four shots and immediately called the police. When the police arrived, they found Miss Suriani dead and Mr. Esau wounded and unconscious from two bullet wounds, one to the head. He was taken to Jacoby Hospital where his condition was reported as critical. When police arrived at the scene, they found a rambling and incoherent note left by the killer.

At this point, the NYPD started to build a profile of the shooter. The portrait they came up with was one of a seriously disturbed man in his mid- to late-twenties, possibly an army veteran, whose recent rejection by young women or possibly his mother's rejection years ago, was contributing to his aberrant behaviour. Police were certain that when he killed his feeling of gratification was temporary and that after a period of days or week cooling down, the emotional pressure inside of him began building up again to the point where he gave in to retaliatory rage. The note left at the scene was said by police to be rambling and incoherent with a taunting tone, although authorities refused to detail its message. In spite of the note and descriptions provided by some of the survivors, police claimed, at least publicly, they had little to go on and were still at the stage of doing such fundamental investigations, such as sifting through records of known sexual offenders.

Soon there was a seventh attack. Two victims were shot at approximately 3:20 A.M. on June 27, 1977. Judy Placido of the Bronx and Sal Lupo of Maspeth, Queens left Elephas Disco around 3:10 A.M. to have a cigarette in a car which was owned by the bartender at Elephas. It was parked by the disco. They were sitting in the car for about 10 minutes having a smoke and a chat. Ironically, they were talking about the .44 caliber killer when the shots rang out. Miss Placido was shot in the right temple, shoulder, and back of the neck. Sal Lupo was shot in his right forearm. After they were shot, Sal Lupo ran back to Elephas to get help. Judy, who was more severely injured, struggled out of the car and staggered a few feet before she collapsed. Both victims were taken to Flushing hospital. Judy was in critical condition, while Sal was listed as in stable condition.

Two witnesses near the scene of the shooting told the police that they saw a dark-haired man dressed in a beige leisure suit jump in a car and hurriedly drive off after the crime. Other witnesses reported a tall, stocky man sprinting from the area, and a blonde man with a moustache, who drove away in a gold Chevy Nova without turning on its headlights. Police speculated the dark-haired man was the shooter and the blonde man had observed the crime and had driven off in a panic.

Capt. Joseph Borelli of the homicide task force said that one witness was also able to see part of the car's license plate. However, Capt. Borelli said, "we cannot say at this point whether that man had anything to do with the shootings." The NYPD never released the partial plate number. Another witness, Borelli said, saw a tall man with a beige leisure suit flee from the scene about the time of the shooting.

Like most of the killers' other victims, Miss Placido had long brown hair. She had celebrated her graduation that day from St. Catherine's Academy in the Bronx. Interestingly,

Valentina Suriani, who was the sixth victim, also attended St. Catherine's Academy in the Bronx. Judy lived in the Pelham Bay section of the Bronx, as did Valentina Suriani and the first victims, Donna Lauria and Jody Valenti. The police tended to dismiss these connections as coincidence since none of the other victims fit that pattern and it wasn't thought the killer was looking for specific people to kill. "We believe he is a killer of opportunity," said Deputy Insp. Timothy Dowd, who was in charge of Operation Omega.

In another interesting twist, a week before the Elephas shooting, an officer at the 111th precinct in Bayside received a phone call from a man stating "this is the Son of Sam. Next week I'm going to hit Bayside." Police took the threat seriously and patrols were increased throughout the precinct, one which was already plagued by a series of muggings, rapes, and other crimes. But as one police supervisor pointed out, "we can't cover all the discos, nightclubs, and bars." It was unclear if the case had moved forward at all as a result of the latest shootings. If the police had any new leads, they were not talking about it.

Customers who were at the disco tried to get help after the shooting, but it took them about 15 minutes to reach the 911 emergency number. Because of this, two of the patrons, one of them an off-duty cop, ran three blocks to the 111th precinct to report the shootings. Deputy Commissioner Francis J. McLoughlin, said the Saturday night and early Sunday morning period was the busiest for emergency calls, and that calls were backed up. However, Deputy Inspector Timothy Dowd pointed out that the squad had arrived on the scene within two minutes of the first radio report Sunday morning.

Ballistics were able to determine that once again, .44 caliber ammunition was used in the shooting. The NYPD was done playing around and requested a list of all .44 caliber permit holders in the city.

They still had no serious suspects. The day after the shooting, a psychiatric patient was held for questioning after he was stopped on the grounds of the Veterans Hospital in Northport while driving a stolen car. He seemed to resemble the composite police sketch, but he was later discounted as a suspect.

Detective Joe Coffey and his partner, George Moscardini, had been patrolling in the vicinity of the Elephas Disco at 2:45 A.M. In an interview, Detective Joe Coffey claimed that almost immediately after the shooting, someone who in hindsight may have possibly been the shooter was walking back to his car. Unaware of the shooting at this time, Coffey stopped him because he seemed suspicious. The person of interest was carrying a brown paper bag. At that point, Coffey received a radio call about the shooting and let the suspect leave the scene. Another coincidence? NYPD might have had the shooter or an accomplice in their grasp, but it wasn't meant to be.

The eighth shooting occurred on July 31, 1977. Stacy Moskowitz and Robert Violante were sitting in a parked car on Shore Road in Brooklyn across the street from a park at approximately 2:50 A.M. The couple did not see the gunman approach the car, but witnesses, including a man who watched it all unfold from the rearview mirror of his car, said the assailant crouched, aimed with both hands and fired 4 shots through the open window in the passenger side. Each victim was shot in the head, Violante once and Moskowitz twice. Mr. Violante sounded his car horn to attract help, and witnesses said he staggered out of the vehicle screaming "help me, don't let me die." The assailant, in the meantime, was said to have walked away calmly across the street, past a playground and into the park, vanishing near the spot where he had appeared. Some witnesses said that a yellow Volkswagen was seen leaving the area shortly after the shooting. A police contingency plan, dubbed "code 44" was put into effect immediately after the shooting was reported.

Police patrols saturated the Bath Beach area and halted lone male motorists, but the effort proved futile. I'm sure the intentions were good setting up this "Code 44" but what if, just by chance, the shooter had an accomplice, a getaway driver? They would have been waved on by the police because they didn't fit what the police were looking for.

The victims were taken to Coney Island Hospital and then transferred to Kings County where both underwent extensive operations. Doctors later said Moskowitz suffered brain damage from a bullet that passed through her head and lodged in her neck. They listed her chances of survival at 50 percent. Violantes' survival chances were said to be better, but he wasn't unscathed. A bullet had passed through his head, destroying his left eye and damaging his right eye. One bullet fired in the attack had lodged in the car's steering column, but the fragment was too badly mangled for ballistics experts to say definitively that it had come from a .44 caliber gun. It was not until surgeons removed nearly a whole bullet from Miss Moskowitz' neck that the police could say that the Son of Sam had struck again. But even before the bullet was analysed, Chief of Detectives John F. Keenan and other police officials said they were nearly certain that the attack had been mounted by the Son of Sam.

Who else could it have been? The pattern of crime certainly seemed to fit, a gun assault in the early morning hours on a weekend night with a young woman with long hair seated in a car with a friend as a victim. Specifically, the number of shots fired also seemed to fit. The Son of Sam killer had in each of the seven previous assaults fired four shots from his five round .44 caliber Charter Arms Bulldog Revolver. Except for the 7:00 P.M. shooting of Virginia Voskerichian, where a single bullet killed her. The time of her attack, number of bullets, and the day of the week (Tuesday) broke the established pattern. The description of the assailant also pointed towards the Son of Sam. Witnesses described a man in his twenties, 5 feet 7 in to 5 feet 10 inches tall, medium build, and dressed casually in dungarees and a grey shirt with the sleeves rolled up.

The police were getting desperate. Despite the efforts of a special task force of 70 detectives who had worked on the case full time since April, the police conceded they were experiencing mounting frustrations and a dearth of leads in recent days. On August 1 at 11 P.M., Mayor Beame told Police Commissioner Michael Codd to assign 100 more policemen to the case. They had to find this killer, and soon. The death toll was rising and as it did the pressure on city officials and law enforcement rose along with it.

Expectations that the killer would strike again ran high on Friday, the anniversary of the July 29, 1976 killing of 18-year-old Donna Lauria, who was his first victim. In one of two taunting notes in recent months, one to the police and one to Jimmy Breslin, *NY Daily News* columnist, the killer asked, "What will you have for July 29? You must not forget Donna Lauria. She is a very sweet girl but Sam's a thirsty lad and he won't let me stop killing until he gets his fill of blood." A detective in the 62nd precinct which covers the Bath Beach section of Brooklyn where Son of Sam attacked Moskowitz and Violante, said that an anonymous caller to the police last week had warned of an approaching strike in Coney Island. While extra patrols were assigned to that area, there were no extra patrols in the area where the shooting actually took place.

Seven

Like everyone else in the New York Area, and even across the country, Maury Terry was following the Son of Sam case closely. His interest wasn't purely personal, to him the case was an obsession. He started writing features about the shootings for the Westchester Journal soon after David Berkowitz was arrested. It wasn't like he had a lot of inside information to work with when he put together his stories. During the shooting spree and for the following two years until Berkowitz had a court hearing, the only information available to Maury, the victims, and the general public was what was printed in the local newspapers. Most people, including myself, had no reason to believe what we heard from the NYPD and read in the three New York newspapers, was anything but true. It's easy to forget, but before the Internet, people had very limited ways to get information.

There were huge discrepancies in what was reported, including, but not limited to, nine police sketches of the suspect that were plastered all over the papers, most of which looked nothing alike. This is the biggest piece of evidence of all that David Berkowitz didn't act alone. He just didn't look like the person that many witnesses described. "The descriptions are so varied," the *New York Times* reported the week before Berkowitz's arrest, "that the police are now considering the possibility that the killer wears various disguises…and has gained weight to complicate further his identification."

Because of this and a few other things that didn't make sense to him, Maury started to question the official law enforcement narrative and, in his opinion, it just didn't add up. It became something he started investigating on his own, and before long, it was his life's work.

He spent the next 10 years tirelessly researching the case which culminated in the publication of the best-selling book, *"The Ultimate Evil."* His book outlined a massive conspiracy that involved several dozen people from David Berkowitz's hometown in Yonkers, all five boroughs of NYC; Long Island; Westchester County (NY); as well as Minot, ND; Houston, TX; and California.

As I wrote previously, I am not attempting to finish Maury Terry's final chapter of *The Ultimate Evil*, but I do want to touch upon some highlights of the book, especially for anyone who hasn't read it. When the book was published 11 years after my getting shot, I too had some questions as to David Berkowitz's guilt. Reading *The Ultimate Evil* answered several of my questions, but also created a thousand more.

The basic premise of *The Ultimate Evil* is that a cult called the 22 Disciples of Hell were the perpetrators of the attacks and Berkowitz was nothing but a lower member of the cult who was following orders and took the fall for the crimes. The "foot soldiers" in the cult, of which Berkowitz was one, answered to a higher group of leaders. At its core, the cult were Satanists, and not the cartoonish, Church of Satan types of Satanist either. These guys were into some bad stuff.

It appeared to Maury their main interest was pedophilia, but they were involved in a myriad of criminal activities. Speaking with law enforcement officials, residents of Yonkers, prison informants, and even some ex-members of the loosely knit cult, Maury was able to piece together what he felt was a conspiracy surrounding the Son of Sam killings. As with any case that was 45 years old, vital information came in at different times, and sometimes changed the initial narrative. Trying to separate what the police reported originally, the newspaper articles that continually reported news based on new information, and the information that Maury uncovered over a period of years is difficult, if not impossible, to put into a neat timeline.

In Maury's introduction to the book, he stated that *The Ultimate Evil* is not simply a Son of Sam story, but rather a search for the nameless forces behind the .44 caliber shootings and numerous other deaths, not only in New York, but across the nation. To complicate the case, and specifically the information Maury put out there with the release of *The Ultimate Evil,* any information he came up with no matter how sound was usually rebuffed by the NYPD and psychiatrists who interviewed David Berkowitz before his trial who refused to believe that a conspiracy existed. Most of these people never questioned David about it. In their opinion, they had their man, why make things more complicated than they needed to be?

A combination of inaccurate reporting, and assumptions made by law enforcement, the press, and so-called criminal profilers, who in this case put together a cookie cutter profile of a serial killer, all fit the narrative that David Berkowitz was the lone killer. Lastly, David Berkowitz was part of the problem also. He changed his story several times before his hearing and then changed his story several more times while in prison. Why should anyone trust him? And the thing is, no one should. But with the corroborating evidence, what Berkowitz has to say means a lot.

A man who Maury called "Brother John" was his first informant that was a part of the cult. He had grown up in Yonkers and went to school with the Carr brothers. According to John, he was pimped out at the tender age of 15 years by a man known as Deuce who operated around 42nd Street in Manhattan trafficking teenagers to businessmen, politicians, and other pedophiles. Brother John had become involved with the cult in the 1960s, but in 1970 he realized that the Untermeyer Park group of devil worshippers were getting strange, even for him. That, coupled with his desire not to be used as a sex toy, prompted him to leave the Untermeyer crowd and move to Manhattan. Over a period of time, Brother John fed Maury information about the cult members, the rituals, and the men who paid dues to provide the boys to the pedophiles. Brother John's information put Maury on the trail of identifying some of the players in the cult who he would not have known about otherwise.

Clues in the letters that were dropped at the Esau/Suriani shooting and the letter mailed to *NY Daily News* columnist, Jimmy Breslin, also helped paint a picture for Maury. Most of the information Brother John provided was corroborated by NYP Detective Jim Rothstein. His sources on 42nd Street actually alerted him to the satanic rituals and the trafficking of boys for sex in Untermeyer Park in 1970, six years before the Son of Sam shooting took place. With the information about John and Michael Carr supplied by Brother John, Maury started investigating their background and lifestyle. John Carr was living in Minot, ND, and was recently discharged from the Air Force. Detectives in Minot told Maury that a group of devil worshippers were very active in the area. Several of John Carr's friends admitted to the Minot detectives that John was involved with a satanic cult and that David Berkowitz had visited John, who had referred to him as "Berky." Another friend of John Carr's was identified by Maury as Larry Milenko*,[1] who was also allegedly involved in the cult activities.

As per Maury's research, the cult in Yonkers and Westchester region began in the 1950s. Back then, when it came to the cult's activity there was a lot of ritual magic, some drugs, and of course, sex with kids—usually boys. According to Maury, it was started by a now-deceased eye

---

1. pseudonym

doctor out of Yonkers. Its early members included some perverse lawyers, a Yonkers judge, and other professionals, along with a handful of working-class youths. The satanism aspect started much later, around 1970, which was when the Process Church became a part of it.

Brother John told Maury about an alleged shooting/ suicide in Van Cortland Park in the North Bronx. According to Brother John, it wasn't suicide at all, but murder. The victim was a young high school teacher by the name of Karen Wahlstrom who he said knew too much about the group. The murder occurred in April of 1965.

Brother John informed Maury about allegations there were missing kid's bodies purported to be buried in Untermeyer Park. Allegedly they were runaways and orphans who wouldn't be missed. In theory, the cult had contacts at orphanages and homes for troubled kids and also used a number of pimps who they paid to pick up boys in the Times Square area.

Brother John heard this information from John Carr in the summer of 1972 when they had a prearranged meeting in O'Henry's Bar in Greenwich Village. Brother John and John Carr had not seen each other for a number of years and, as they talked, John Carr began to tell him what had been going on at Untermeyer. Brother John said John Carr was very upset when he talked about the bodies said to be buried in Untermeyer Park. He also stated new leadership had taken over the group and that he might soon have to kill someone. This meeting was not long after the Process merged with the pre-existing Westchester/Yonkers satanic group. Other ties to the cult would soon emerge in Connecticut, the Hamptons on Long Island, Texas, and North Dakota. The cult met at three places in Untermeyer Park. The Devil's Cave, the Eagle's Nest, and the Old Caretakers Stonehouse down on the Aqueduct.

At one point, Maury met a teenager who he calls "Billy the Artist." Billy had met some of the group at the Eagle's

Nest in June 1976. The Artist drew very good caricatures of a handful of the cult members which Maury was able to see. One of the portraits depicted a cult member known as "Ken from Australia." Another drawing was of a pretty young woman Maury called Suzette Rodriguez (aka Maria Cortina), who would be murdered in Elmsford, NY, not far from Yonkers, a few months after Berkowitz' arrest. The artist drew Maria crying. He said it was because "Ken from Australia" who was also a member, had been yelling at her. The artist also drew a man known as Mr. Real Estate, a top leader of the cult who hardly ever appeared at Untermeyer. Years later, the artist positively identified him in his coffin when cops took him to Mr. Real Estate's wake in 1996.

Many years later, Yonkers Police learned that the night of the Berkowitz arrest a somewhat panicked meeting of several local cult members was held at the JFK marina on the Yonkers waterfront. It was known to cult members that Berkowitz planned to claim sole responsibility for the shootings, but they wanted to be ready to have a contingency plan just in case he dropped the ball.

Also, of great importance to prove the theory of Berkowitz not acting alone, but something that has hardly been given any attention to, is that the bullets that Berkowitz had in his possession were not the bullets he purchased in Houston, Texas in June of 1976. His gun was initially acquired by Berkowitz through an old Army friend, Billy Daniel Parker, on June 12, 1976, in a Houston, Texas gun shop. The original ammo purchased in Houston vanished and other bullets ended up in Berkowitz' apartment. Besides the distinct possibility others were using Berkowitz's gun, it is very likely other .44s were used as well, especially in the earlier attacks. This was before NYPD announced they believed, despite evidence to the contrary, that one person had been doing all the shootings. The truth is they were muddled, confused, and unclear about what was happening in all the incidents right from the start. This fact was also stated by the Queens DA, John Santucci.

Berkowitz also confirmed a 1977 police report in which a witness said Berkowitz was seen at 1147 First Avenue, the main location of the Process Church in Manhattan with one of the founders of the Process, "Father Lars."

This is just some of the information Maury uncovered that pointed to multiple people being involved. When Maury first started investigating, so many things about the official narrative didn't add up, and as the years went on, it became more and more obvious that there was much still to be discovered. While much of this information is circumstantial, when it is all put together there is little doubt that much of it holds water.

Pictures

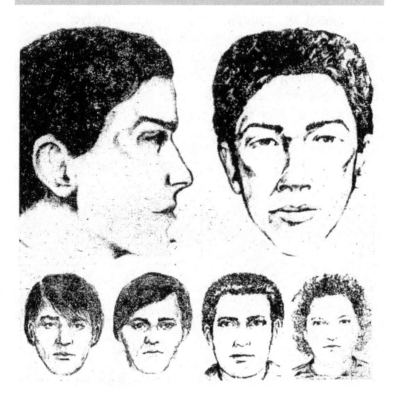

*Numerous sketches of suspects making it
obvious there is more than one suspect.*

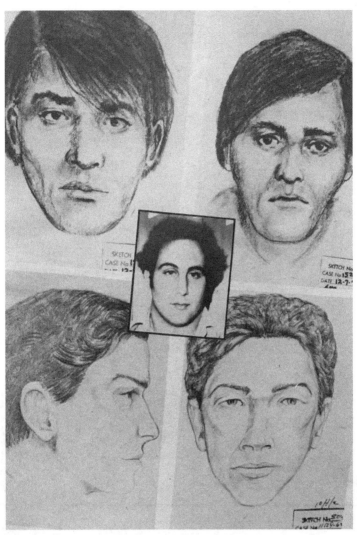

*This photo makes it obvious Berkowitz was
not the only person being described.*

The Lomino/DeMasi shooter.

Another police sketch that looks nothing like Berkowitz.

Pecks Bar and Grill

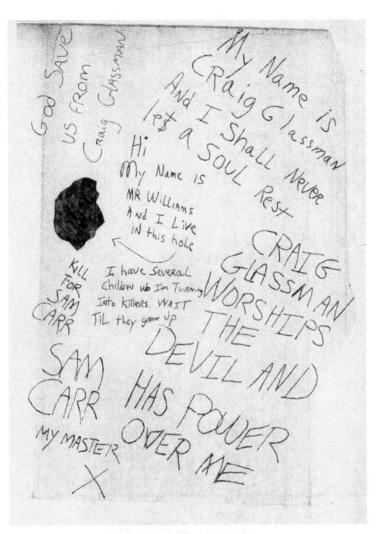

*The wall in the apartment of Berkowitz
after he was arrested.*

A check for the infamous parking ticket.

Maury Terry

Maury and Berkowitz

Me in younger days.

A photo of the car I was shot in.

Me today.

I SAY GOODBYE AND
GOODNIGHT.

POLICE - LET ME
HAUNT YOU WITH THESE
WORDS;

I'LL BE BACK!
I'LL BE BACK!

TO BE INTERRPRETED
AS - BANG, BANG, BANG,
BANK, BANG - UGH!!

YOURS IN
MURDER

MR. MONSTER

Letter found near the bodies of Esau and Suriani. The handwriting is much different than Breslin letter.

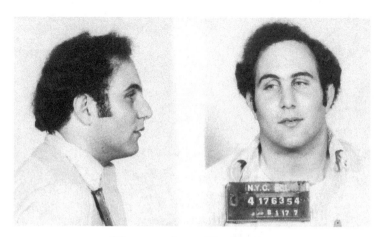

The mugshot of Berkowitz.

Promotional Material for Process Church

NOT KNOWING WHAT THE FUTURE
HOLDS I SHALL SAY FAREWELL AND
I WILL SEE YOU AT THE NEXT JOB.
OR SHOULD I SAY YOU WILL SEE
MY HANDIWORK AT THE NEXT JOB?
REMEMBER MS. LAURIA. THANK YOU.

IN THEIR BLOOD
AND
FROM THE GUTTER

"SAM'S CREATION". 44

HERE ARE SOME NAMES TO HELP YOU ALONG.
FORWARD THEM TO THE INSPECTOR FOR
USE BY N.C.I.C.:
"THE DUKE OF DEATH"
"THE WICKED KING WICKER"
"THE TWENTY TWO DISCIPLES OF HELL"
"JOHN 'WHEATIES' - RAPIST AND SUFF-
OCATER OF YOUNG GIRLS.

PS: J.B. PLEASE INFORM ALL THE
DETECTIVES WORKING THE
SLAYINGS TO REMAIN

Breslin letter.

Untermyer Park

Eight

In this book, I have previously recapped the official view of all the Son of Sam shootings, which is the version that was reported in newspapers and in press conferences based on reports by law enforcement. In this chapter, I am going to attempt to report all the new information since the shootings first occurred that has been uncovered by the NYPD, as well as what was covered in *The Ultimate Evil.*

I also will present information on the shootings that was uncovered by Maury, myself, and other investigators since the book's publication. Much of this information has never before been reported. While some of what I am about to write may be redundant, I feel it is important to sum up the attacks briefly again, so the information is fresh in your mind when the new information is introduced.

On Thursday evening, at 1:10 A.M. on July 29 of 1976, the .44 caliber killer attacked and shot Donna Lauria and Jody Valenti. This was the first of eight murders or attempted murders by this person or group. Six of the ensuing attacks happened in the early morning hours on the weekend.

The two women went to a disco called The Peach Tree in New Rochelle on Wednesday night. It was established later that members of the Carr family, who according to Maury's research were firmly entrenched in the cult and possible triggermen occasionally patronized the Peach Tree. Earlier that evening, a yellow compact car was seen cruising Donna's block before she went out that night. Later that evening when Donna's father, Mike Lauria, came home, he saw a light tan Ford occupied by a lone male parked behind Jody's car across the street from their apartment building.

A confidential police report mentioned that a male acquaintance of Donna's was quoted by a young woman Donna knew as saying that "Donna has one week to live." The NYPD didn't completely disregard this piece of information. The man in question, "Vinny" had been Donna's boyfriend, but they recently broke up. Vinny became a prime suspect until he provided an alibi and Jody Valenti came out and said he wasn't the gunman. Besides being Donna's ex-boyfriend, Vinny owned a .44 caliber handgun and worked in the pornography business, allegedly with the Gambino crime family.

Berkowitz didn't act alone during this shooting. Three other people were at the scene in addition to David Berkowitz. Maury later got the information that Michael Carr was there that night from Berkowitz himself.

Berkowitz also said that parked across the street in a light tan car, the one that was observed by Lauria's father, sat two other accomplices. According to Berkowitz, one of the two was a then-Yonkers resident named "Richie" and the other was Gorman Johnson*. [2] Later Maury discovered that the tan Ford was a car service vehicle registered in the name of Gorman Johnson's wife. Gorman Johnson also owned a .44 bulldog revolver and in 1977 lived near Berkowitz in Yonkers. This tan Ford was seen at a few other Son of Sam shooting sites. In July 1977, nine days before the Moskowitz/Violante attack in Brooklyn, Yonkers police caught Gorman Johnson as he was trying to ditch that very same tan Ford in the Hudson River.

Jody Valenti gave the NYPD a description of the gunman: He was a white male in his 30s, around 5 ft 9 inches tall, and weighing 160 lbs, with dark curly hair. He

---

2. Pseudonym

was clean shaven, with a light complexion, and wearing a blue polo shirt with white stripes. Jody described the gun used to shoot her as a long-barrelled, wild west-type gun. This description matches the physical appearance of David Berkowitz. He admitted to being the shooter of this attack. However, the gun she described is in sharp contrast to the .44 caliber Charter Arms Bulldog revolver that the NYPD eventually said was the gun used in the attack.

The second attack, October 23, 1976 was when me and Rosemary Keenan were shot at on 159th Street and 33rd Avenue in Flushing. There were no witnesses to this attack so there is very little information available outside of what the NYPD gathered from me and Rosemary. Long after *The Ultimate Evil* was published, it was learned by Maury and myself that a relative of Wheat Carr was house-sitting two blocks away from the shooting. Although there is not conclusive proof, it is believed that the relative, Eileen Dorfler, hosted a party that night and some of the attendees were somehow involved in the crime. At the time, her son Glen Dorfler, was 15 years old. Thirty years later he passed away and Wheat Carr posted her condolences on the funeral website, indicating that Glen was her nephew. In another twist, Glen apparently worked for James Faulkner in a local Yonkers TV studio. At one point, James Faulkner purchased the Carr family residence for below market value. In 1993, in a televised interview with Maury, David Berkowitz stated that, although he was at the scene of this attack, he was not the shooter. When pressed by Maury, he admitted that the shooter was a woman. Originally, Maury told me the shooter was a known "witch" named Wendy. In occult circles, she was known as "Big Breasted Wendy." She was also a regular visitor/customer at the Magikal Childe Occult shop in Greenwich Village. About 5 years before Maury's death, he sent me an email saying that the woman who shot me was not Wendy, but was actually a woman named Amy. To this day, I am not sure if the woman that shot me is Wendy or Amy.

Even with a lack of eyewitnesses to the shooting, a bit of circumstantial evidence does exist. The shooter's aim was wild. Four bullets were fired, one piece of shrapnel hit the speedometer of the Volkswagen, one apparently went through the back window and out the front window, blowing the windows out. The third bullet hit the roof of the car which slowed the bullet down, it eventually found its resting spot in the back of my skull. After the attack, Rosemary's Volkswagen was towed to the police garage for further investigation. A week later when the NYPD returned Rosemary's car, she went to clean it out and pulled a blanket from the rear wheel well of the Beetle, and lo and behold, a bullet fell out. She immediately gave her father, Detective Red Keenan, the bullet and it was sent to ballistics. I'm not really sure which bullet determined it was a .44 caliber— that bullet or the bullet the doctors took out of my skull, but regardless, it was one of them.

In the early 1990s, I met with Detective Joe Quirk who worked in ballistics in the NYPD. He told me that he worked on my case and based on his findings, he reported that it was either a 90-pound weakling or a woman who fired the shots in my attack. In the 1993 interview, when David Berkowitz admitted to Maury Terry that a woman shot me, the detective's statement was corroborated. The detective also told me during our conversation that the ballistics report he worked on was missing from the NYPD files.

Martin Bracken, ADA from Queens, met with David Berkowitz in the early morning hours of August 11, 1977. He questioned Berkowitz about my shooting and where I was, which was thought to be sitting in the passenger seat of a navy blue VW Beetle. Berkowitz incorrectly stated that the car was red. He also stated that he fired 5 times at the car and that he intended to kill "just the woman. I thought she was in the front seat passenger side. It was very dark."

The remainder of the questioning about this attack was sketchy and Berkowitz's answers were brief and apparently semi-factual. But the damage was done. For someone who apparently shot me, he didn't seem to know a whole lot about it.

The third attack was on November 27, 1976 when Joanne Lomino and Donna DeMasi were shot in Floral Park, Queens. The biggest piece of circumstantial evidence from this shooting was the police sketch that was developed by the NYPD based on the victim's description of the shooter. Two sketches of the shooter were drawn by the NYPD. Both were similar except for the part in the shooter's hair. One sketch showed the shooter with a left part, the other with a right part. Other than that, the sketches were identical. These sketches didn't look a thing like Berkowitz. Not even a little bit.

In a report from a witness who didn't see the shooting but saw the gunman running away from the scene of the crime, the witness said the shooter was carrying a weapon in his left hand. Berkowitz was right-handed. Berkowitz also stated later that the women were running up the steps when he shot them. However, Joanne Lomino stated to the prosecutors that "we were standing by the sidewalk talking. We walked over to the porch and we were standing for about 5 minutes. I heard a voice, we turned around and a guy pulled a gun and started shooting at us." Berkowitz also stated in his confession that the victims were face to face with him. Joanne Lomino was fired upon first and was shot in the back. She further stated, "I had my back turned towards him and he just had the gun out and fired it. My back was towards him though." This is more obvious proof that Berkowitz wasn't the shooter as he didn't know details of the crime.

All the more interesting, both sketches appear to be the spitting image of John Carr. Linda O'Connor, John Carr's girlfriend, has stated that John Carr was in New York at the time of the attacks on Joanne Lomino and Donna DeMasi, as well as three other Son of Sam shootings. He was eliminated as a suspect in the October 23rd wounding of myself and the murders of Virginia Voskerichian, Valentina Suriana, and Alex Esau. Another strong piece of evidence linking Carr to the Son of Sam case was the discovery by Maury that Carr dated 13-15-year-old girls when he lived in Minot, North Dakota. Two friends, including Tom Keller and Frank Head reported this proclivity to Maury. Remember, in the Breslin letter, John Wheaties was called a "rapist and suffocater of young girls." Minot, North Dakota detective Terry Gardner told Maury an informant stated that Carr advised her that "a chain of safe houses for Satanists on the run existed in the United States and Canada." Detective Gardner checked with the Canadian authorities and was told that there was some kind of network of safe houses that existed for bikers and they heard that it was possible that Satanists also sometimes used the facilities. To top all this off, John Carr was truly a Son of Sam, as his father was named Sam Carr.

Over time, David Berkowitz admitted that several members of the cult were present at all of the shooting scenes. In addition, the group usually had a safe house nearby for them to go to and hide out in the event that it was needed. In the Lomino/DeMasi shooting, David Berkowitz' sister, whom he was in contact with during the Son of Sam attacks, lived in Glen Oaks, about ten blocks from the shooting. Additionally, the well-known photographer, Robert Mapplethorpe's family lived about three blocks from the shooting attack. There is circumstantial evidence, including an audio tape made by a former roommate of Mapplethorpe that Mapplethorpe hired Ron Sisman to videotape the Violante/Moskowitz scene at the request of Roy Radin. Sisman was later murdered under mysterious circumstances. Radin was later murdered by contract killer William Mentzer, who Maury felt was deeply involved in the cult's sinister dealings. I will write more of that later in this chapter.

And the killings continued. Two years after Berkowitz' arrest, John Carr met an untimely death when he was killed with a shotgun blast to his face. Interestingly, Detective Gardner called Michael Carr, instead of Sam Carr, to tell him of John's death. Linda O'Connor told Detective Gardner not to call Sam Carr to tell him about it because he had a heart condition. Also of interest is that there was mention in the letter to Breslin about Papa Sam's heart condition. Another player in this saga is a man Maury called Reeve Rockman*.[3]

Although it is not known if he was actually at any of the attacks, it is known that he lived in Queens, was good friends with John Carr, and had visited Carr several times in North Dakota. Several of John Carr's friends, including his girlfriend, said that Reeve Rockman and John Carr dealt drugs in New York. Two of Carr's North Dakota friends said Carr carried a photo of Reeve Rockman in his wallet and told them "this is the guy who wants to kill me."

The fourth attack was perpetrated on Christine Freund and John Diel on January 30, 1977 at around 12:40 A.M. Unlike the previous shooting, there were no eyewitnesses to this attack. The ballistics test failed to link the bullets fired at Freund to any other shooting. But it was noted that a .44 caliber weapon identified as a Charter Arms Bulldog Revolver had been used to fire upon the victims. The police used the composite sketch from the Lauria and the Lomino/ DeMasi shootings to try to find the perpetrator of the Freund and Diel shooting and, as I made clear previously, the composite sketch did not match David Berkowitz.

In *The Ultimate Evil*, Maury reported that the shooter was from "the west coast" and was brought in by the cult to do the shooting. During one of Maury Terry's jailhouse interviews with Berkowitz, he stated that the guy that was

---

3. Pseudonym

brought in from the west coast had something to do with the Manson family in California. Maury identified the shooter as "Manson II." Later it was revealed that Manson II was Bill Mentzer. In 1991, Mentzer was tried and convicted in the 1983 murder of Roy Radin and the 1984 murder of June Mincher. He was sentenced to life in prison without parole. He is serving his sentence in a prison in Lancaster, California. Los Angeles Police Department has openly acknowledged that Mentzer was a member of something that was thought of as "some kind of hit squad." *Post* reporter Jamie Schram interviewed Mentzer when Schram discovered two dozen links between Mentzer and the Zodiac killer. At the end of his interview, Schram nonchalantly asked Mentzer about the Freund shooting and, according to Jamie Schram, his face turned white and he would not respond to the accusation.

It is alleged that Mentzer was brought in to be the killer in the Freund shooting as a warning to Diel who was having an affair with a New York mobster's wife. Unfortunately, if that was the case, it was a case of mistaken identity. John Diel's brother, who was also a bartender and had a similar build, would have actually been the guy they meant to target.

Maury's prison source, "Vinny", told him that Berkowitz said the Diel shooting was a hit and that he was at the shooting scene but was not the shooter. Vinny stated that the shooting was a message to John Diel that involved a love triangle between John Diel, Christine Freund, and a married woman. During the course of his investigation, Maury read the NYPD confessions they received from Berkowitz. The story that Berkowitz told the NYPD and the story that he told "Vinny", the prison informant, differed in several aspects from John Diel's story. When Maury approached John Diel several months after the shooting, he asked him if anything strange happened earlier in the evening of the attack. Diel's response to Maury was they (meaning the NYPD) never asked him that question, but yes there was. In the beginning of the evening, Diel dropped Christine off at the movie theatre and went to search for a place to park. When he finally parked his car, he noticed two men nearby in a light tan or off-white compact car, the size of a Chevy Nova. The passenger in the compact car jumped out and leaned against its opened door. He appeared to be thin, had dirty blonde, styled hair, that looked to be blow dried, and was in his early twenties. When Diel got out of the car and began to go towards the theatre, the passenger got back in the car, and the car drove away.

After the movie, Chris and John went to the Wine Gallery for a few drinks. Christine noticed two guys at the bar that she described to John as creepy looking. One had brown hair and severe acne on his face, the other had sandy brown hair parted in the center and appeared to be in his thirties. Outside the restaurant, Diel ran into a man he later positively identified as David Berkowitz. Berkowitz was dressed in a beige raincoat which is the same garment he was seen wearing two weeks later at the Voskerichian murder. Diel and Freund started the trek back to the car, which was about a quarter mile away. The shooting occurred several minutes after they got in the car. In another strange twist, Berkowitz confessed to the NYPD that he was about four or five feet away from the couple as they entered the car, claiming he was able to watch from such a close distance because he hid behind a tree. The only problem with that statement is there are no trees on the block where the shooting occurred. Berkowitz also stated that he approached the car from the rear, but in order to do this, he would have to walk past the car. John Diel swears that no one passed the car during this time period.

The description of the two men that Christine and John saw at the Wine Gallery closely matches the description that Vinny reported of Manson II and one of his associates. Vinny's portrayal of Manson II also matched that of the man who reportedly watched the shooting at Elephas and drove off in a yellow car with his lights extinguished. Vinny also stated, "Berkowitz knew that the Freund shooting was a hit", but he said he didn't know the motive.

John Diel acknowledged to Maury Terry that he was in love with Christine, but he wasn't faithful to her as he admitted having several affairs. Diel classified two of the affairs as one-nighters, but the third one, a married woman Diel was having sex with, was more serious. Christine found out Diel was seeing someone else when she found a love letter from the woman. After laying down the law to Diel, Chris mailed a note to the married woman (police found a draft copy and the woman's reply) threatening to expose the relationship to her husband.

This doesn't prove conclusively that it was a hit on Christine and a warning to Diel, but the NYPD spent weeks interviewing Christine's friends about the affair and the letter and, eventually, the woman in question herself. Strangely, that investigation ended abruptly with the shooting of Virginia Voskerichian, which was just blocks away from the Freund attack. It is also odd that the NYPD, who interviewed John Diel extensively about the shooting, never asked him if anything strange had happened a week before or earlier in the evening of the shooting.

This wasn't the first time the NYPD was investigating a shooting and dropped part of the investigation when it didn't fit their narrative. The fifth attack was perpetrated on Virginia Voskerichian on March 8, 1977 at around 7:30 P.M. While coming home from Columbia University, Virginia exited the subway at Continental Ave in Forest Hills at about 7:25 P.M. for her short walk home. About a half hour earlier, a brother and sister were out jogging and ran past a man who the female jogger said made her uncomfortable. She later said he had very eerie eyes and was behaving in a threatening manner. The man wore a beige 3/4 length raincoat, and was about 6 feet tall, with wavy dark hair, and weighed about 175 lbs. The joggers ran past this person around Continental Avenue and Dartmouth Street. Feeling scared, they decided to head back to their home on Exeter Street. As they turned down Exeter, they spotted the same man in the beige coat a block in front of them. The female jogger became even more uptight as she wondered how this man was able to get ahead of them even though they were running the whole time. They got to the front door of their house and saw the man walking away towards Tennis Place and Dartmouth Street. About the same time the two joggers spotted the man in the beige coat walking away, Virginia had started her walk down Dartmouth Street to her home. When she neared 4 Dartmouth Street, Virginia noticed a figure walking towards her wearing a ski cap. She started to veer a little to her left to let the passer-by have some room to pass her on her right. As the person in the ski cap was in five feet of her, he pulled out a gun and pointed it at her face. In an effort to protect herself, she raised her schoolbooks to her face to ward off the coming attack. She was shot in the head and died.

Years later, as I looked at crime photos of the attack taken by the NYPD, I noticed that a very large shoulder bag was on the ground next to Virginia's lifeless body. This might not seem important, but I find it strange that she was carrying her books in her arms and had them at the ready to protect her face. Why would she carry such a large bag and not use it to carry her books? This may mean nothing, but it's worth pondering

While running away from the attack, the shooter pulled the ski hat off as he passed a 59-year-old male witness. The witness said that "ski hat" exclaimed, "Oh Jesus!" and put the ski hat back up in front of his face to avoid being recognized.

The witness saw the killer's face briefly and reported that the person looked like a 16-18-year-old with a stocky build, about 5 ft 7 inches tall, clean shaven, and wore a ski jacket.

When questioned by the Queens District Attorney's office after his arrest, as to what he said when he passed this particular witness, David Berkowitz stated that he said, "Hi Mister" which is quite a far cry from "Oh Jesus." David Berkowitz also stated during his interview he was wearing a ski jacket and a brown ski cap. In actuality, the ski cap was striped, but did have a brown stripe in it.

The Voskerichian shooting raised some other interesting points. The shooting occurred on Tuesday evening, on the early side at 7:30 P.M.. This changed the M.O. of the shooter as the other attacks were done in the early morning hours. Initially the NYPD said there was no connection to the Freund shooting, even though that attack happened about a block away. They also said that the "chubby teenager" was a prime suspect. The bullet that was extracted from Virginia Voskerichian's body at the morgue was tested by the NYPD ballistics team. They were able to identify it as a .44 caliber and that it was fired from a Charter Arms Bulldog Revolver. They now had proof that a .44 caliber revolver was used in the previously- apparently-random shootings in Queens and the Bronx and that a Charter Arms Bulldog Revolver was used in at least two of the shootings.

While investigators were getting closer, what the NYPD didn't have was anything resembling one gun-one shooter evidence. Based on eyewitnesses, police sketches provided by the witnesses, and victims' recollections, the NYPD had produced several sketches of suspects that did not match each other. Of the 17 bullet fragments tested by the NYPD Ballistics Department, two of them were narrowed down as being the bullets fired from a Charter Arms Bulldog revolver that killed Donna Lauria and Virginia Voskerichian.

On March 10, 1977, two days after the Voskerichian murder, the NYPD and Mayor Beam convened a press conference to publicly state there was a ballistics match between the Lauria and the Voskerichian bullets, and they could say that both were fired from the same .44 revolver. This made it probable that the same gun was used in those two attacks, but even so there was no evidence pointing to a single individual acting alone. They would also further allege that although tests results weren't as definitive, they were nonetheless "certain" that the bullets used in the Denaro, Lomino/DeMasi, and Freund cases were from the same gun, and the killer in each was the same man. Of course, they had no proof of the latter, but the pressure on law enforcement to make progress on this case was intense and growing by the day.

The press conference was held at the 112th precinct in Forest Hills where NYPD Commissioner Michael Codd and Mayor Beam proclaimed the birth of the ".44 caliber killer." Commissioner Codd and Mayor Beam took great pains to impart the message that the murdering .44 fiend was "NOT the man in the ski cap." The ski cap suspect was still wanted for questioning, but Codd revealed that his men were primarily seeking a white male, about 6 ft tall, 180 lbs., wearing a beige raincoat, and with dark straight hair brushed straight back. Incidentally, this was the description the two joggers gave to the police of the man who frightened them shortly before the shots were fired. It was never released to the public. The next day, the *NY Times* reported: "Mayor Beam and Police Commissioner Codd, in a joint appeal to the public for help, disclosed yesterday that the police were seeking the same man for the senseless killings of three young women since July 29, 1976, including two recently from Forest Hills."

The Commissioner gave the following description of the person wanted for questioning in the murders: He was male, white, between 25 and 30 years of age, between 5 ft 10 in and 6 ft tall, medium build, well-groomed, with dark hair, straight, combed straight back. When asked if this could be the murderer, Commissioner Codd said, "I can't say he is a suspect." Interestingly, the press never pressured Codd about the ski cap suspect from the previous two days, and the fact that the descriptions he gave to the public were so different.

In another twist, the same day as the *NY Times* article appeared, the *Daily News* also reported on the story. The *Daily News* piece was basically the same story that the *Times* reported, but the *Daily News* included a quote from Commissioner Codd's press conference where he said ballistics established the same .44 caliber "wild west" type of revolver had been used in all five shootings.

When people researched Virginia Voskerichian's background, they uncovered the fact that she was dating one of her professors at Columbia. While connecting the dots, Maury discovered that the professor lived near the scene of the crime and frequented the River Run Bookstore in Hastings. Ironically, Dr. Carleton Gadjusek was a frequent visitor to the same bookstore. Dr. Gadjusek, who lived in Yonkers, was a convicted pedophile and also a Nobel prize winner in 1976.

The sixth attack involved Valentina Suriani and Alexander Esau and happened on April 17, 1977 around 3:30 A.M. This attack had no eyewitnesses but was nonetheless a turning point in the .44 caliber killer case. During David Berkowitz's interrogation, he told police that he parked his car on the shoulder of the Hutchinson River Parkway, walked uphill to the service road, and fired his gun from the passenger's side of the car containing the victims, killing both Suriani and Esau. Ironically, the shooting occurred about a block away from Valentina's home, and right across the street from Jody Valenti's house. In this attack, the shooter was very accurate. The NYPD stated that they found an envelope addressed to Borelli in the middle of the street. Inside the envelope was the letter which gave birth to the "Son of Sam."

The day after the shooting, the *Daily News* headlines screamed "KILLER TO COPS - I'LL DO IT AGAIN. TAUNTING NOTE IS FIRST SOLID CLUE." Beneath the headline were two composite sketches, both from the Voskerichian murder which happened in March. One sketch was the ski cap suspect, and the other was the man in the beige raincoat suspect. As the police had already claimed only one man was behind the killings, they were now publicly naming the man in the ski cap as a witness.

The *Daily News*, quoting a police source, said the letter advised authorities that the murderer "lived in a nightmare world of blood-sucking vampires and Frankenstein monsters." The news also reported that the letter contained words in "a Scottish accent" and the phrase "too many heart attacks." This wording would set police pouring through hospital records because they believed it was possible that the killer's father might have been mistreated by brown-haired nurses after suffering cardiac arrest. Donna Lauria and Jody Valenti were in the medical field and this helped fuel that theory. This is a strange assumption by the NYPD as they previously stated that the victims were randomly chosen by the killer.

The people of New York never knew why authorities entertained these thoughts because the note was withheld from the public. The media was also in the dark. The *Daily News* hadn't had access to it either and so the police were able to deny, falsely, that the assassin warned he would strike again. Strangely, the rank-and-file members of the task force didn't view the correspondence, as several of the members stated years later. Withholding the Borelli letter seems to be a significant error on the part of investigators because the note contained important clues, which, if released, might have led to an arrest months sooner which could have meant there were fewer victims. In addition, the letter clearly indicated that an attack had been planned to occur in Queens, rather than the Bronx, and was to have been carried out the week before, around the time of Easter. That is, a shooting scheduled for 7 days earlier in Queens was for some reason delayed and transferred to the Bronx. The evidence was at variance with the official psychological profile of an obsessed murderer whose pent-up internal rages exploded unpredictably. For some reason, only a handful of police officials and consulting psychiatrists would see the shooter's letter, except for Jimmy Breslin, a columnist for the *Daily News*. In fact, Breslin wound end up seeing a note the police wouldn't even share with the detectives working on the case.

On the 26th of May, 1977, the NYPD released a new psychological profile of the killer. Psychiatrists analysing the contents of the letter described the writer as neurotic, schizophrenic, and paranoid. On May 30, 1977, which was Memorial Day, Jimmy Breslin received a letter that was mailed from Englewood, New Jersey. The *Daily News* milked the information in the letter for several days with teasing articles about its contents, meant to build circulation, and it worked. A few days later, the *Daily News* finally published the missive, purportedly from the killer. More than any other effect the release of this letter had, it caused millions of New Yorkers to try to solve the case. Suddenly, everyone was a detective with a theory as to who the killer was. It contained four potential aliases of the killer's names which triggered hundreds of leads in the public's mind. That desire to be a detective and solve the case hasn't stopped. To this day, many people are still spinning, sleuthing, and trying to solve the case. But who am I to talk? I am one of them after all.

In a stark contrast to the Borelli letter, this letter was a masterpiece, graphic, flowing, and literally bubbling with vivid imagery. It was the work of a creative, intelligent writer. Even Breslin remarked that this writer knew how to write and knew his grammar.

On June 26, 1977, Judy Placido and Sal Lupo were shot two blocks from the Elephas Disco in Bayside, Queens. Judy was wounded in the shoulder, the neck, and the head. Sal sustained injuries to his right wrist and had glass fragments slice into his right leg. As per David Berkowitz, Michael Carr was the shooter in this particular crime. A late-60s gold Cadillac with a black vinyl roof was seen cruising the neighbourhood prior to the shooting. The driver had short black hair and a thin moustache.

Ralph Saccente, the bouncer at the Elephas Disco and a friend of Sal promised to drive Judy home to the Bronx after the club had closed. About an hour before closing, Saccente gave Sal the keys to his maroon 1972 Cadillac, and suggested the pair wait in his car until he finished up closing.

Once in the car, Lupo sat in the driver's seat. As they whiled away time, the couple started talking about the Son of Sam case. At around 3:30 am, the conversation was interrupted by gunfire. The attack happened on 211th Street near 45th Avenue in Bayside. After the shooting stopped, Lupo fled the scene, running back towards Elephas. Judy was dazed and not really aware she was wounded until she looked in the rearview mirror and saw she was covered in blood. In a panic, she got out of the car and stumbled down 45th Avenue until she collapsed. A small crowd gathered around her and placed a blanket over her body. In the meantime, Sal had reached Elephas and told the door man about the shooting. Before long, police and ambulances were on the scene arriving at about the same time that Sal returned to Judy.

Interestingly, a week before the shooting occurred, the dispatcher at the 111th precinct, which is about 4 blocks away from Elephas, received an anonymous call from a man stating, "this is the Son of Sam - Bayside is next." Because of this call, the NYPD had beefed up their patrol in the Bayside area. This information was never released to the press or the public. Detective Joe Coffey and his partner were in the vicinity of Elephas looking for suspicious people and activities when the call came over the radio that shots were fired two blocks from Elephas.

Three blocks south of the shooting, a witness observed a stocky white male clad in dark clothing running down 211th Street heading away from the scene of the crime. Another witness saw a well-dressed young man, with sandy-colored hair and a moustache jump into a yellowish or gold Nova-type car and leave the neighborhood with the headlights extinguished. This person was thought to be Michael Carr. It is believed this man watched the shooting and then fled in the same direction as the shooter went. This information was also kept from the press and the public. A similar vehicle was double-parked across the street from the scene of the first Son of Sam shooting, Donna Lauria. The car was registered to Gorman Johnson's wife. The sedan was used by a Bronx car service. Johnson would be caught trying to ditch this car in the Hudson River in July of 1977, but at the time, no one knew it was rumoured to be involved in several SOS shootings. Later, evidence emerged that this car was seen at two other Son of Sam shootings as well.

Both victims recovered from their wounds. When questioned by the police, neither Sal nor Judy could identify the shooter.

There are numerous odd things around this shooting that could be facts involving the case.

Judy lived on a street named Wickham. The words "Wicked King Wicker" had appeared in the Breslin letter, received just days before the attack.

Judy's last name, Placido, is very similar to Placida, who was the protector of the Roman sewers and gutters. The words "sewers" and "gutters" also appeared in the Breslin letter.

Elephas Levi was a 19th century occultist and was also the name of the disco where the victims had been hanging out. Elephas is a Latin word that means elephant and in the occult world the elephant is the demon, Behemoth, which is a reference that appeared in the letter written to Captain Borelli.

The envelope that contained the Breslin letter had a note written on the back of the envelope:

BLOOD AND FAMILY

DARKNESS AND DEATH

ABSOLUTE DEPARAVITY

.44

Underneath that message was the Son of Sam symbol.

This information was also withheld from the public and the press. Eerily, Judy had gone to the funeral of the 6th attack victim, Valentina Suriani. Both had attended St. Catherine's Academy, although they didn't know each other.

The Lupo/Placido shooting occurred at 3:30 am, the latest time any victims were shot. One of the getaway cars used at the shooting scene was driven by "Richie", a cult member who allegedly was an accomplice at the 4th Son of Sam shooting. Richie had received a ticket for parking in a crosswalk near Judy's home a few weeks prior to that attack.

Are these just coincidences? For now, you be the judge.

Nine

On July 28, 1977, *New York Daily News* reporter Jimmy Breslin wrote a column entitled "To the .44 Killer on His First Deathday." In his column, Breslin pontificated as to if and when the Son of Sam would strike again, writing, "And somewhere in this city, a loner, a deranged loner, picks up this paper and gloats. Again, he has what he wants. Is tomorrow, July 29, so significant to him that he must go out and walk the night street and find a victim? Or will he sit alone, and look out his attic window and be thrilled by his power? This power that will have him in the newspapers and on television and in the thoughts and conversations of most of the young people in this city?"

On Saturday, July 30, 1977, Robert Violante went to pick up Stacy Moskowitz at her home in Flatbush, Brooklyn for their first date. Violante parked his father's 1969 brown Buick Skylark and opened the gate to Stacy's front walk. As Stacy was getting ready, Robert and Stacy's parents spent some time chatting and getting to know each other. As they did so, the parents indicated their concern about their daughter going out during the height of the Son of Sam killings. Robert Violante told them not to worry, he would look after their daughter. They were going to see a movie and get something to eat after or maybe go to a disco for a bit. Stacy's mom told her daughter as they were leaving, "Now I want you to have a good time, but remember that Son of Sam." Stacy remarked, "This is Brooklyn, not

Queens. And anyway, I'm a blonde. We'll be just fine." The couple decided to skip having a meal before the 10 o'clock showing of the Martin Scorsese film, *New York, New York*. First, they went to Shore Parkway to a park and spent some time on the swings. Then they drove to Graves End Bay to watch the ships float by in the harbour. After that they drove to the Kingsway Theatre in Coney Island to see the movie. When it ended, they decided to drive back to Shore Parkway and spend some more time together. Apparently, the date was going well.

The time of the shooting, as established by neighbors' calls to the NYPD's 911 emergency number was 2:35 A.M., but the story of the shooting actually began to unfold 90 minutes earlier. At 1:10 A.M., a woman and her husband were searching for her lost bracelet. They had no luck and returned to their car, which was parked on the service road near Bay 16th Street. As the couple were talking in their car, they observed a yellow VW Beetle pull up to the park's entrance and watched two people emerge from the car and walk into the park. At about 1:30 A.M., Dominic Spagnola parked on the south side of the Shore Parkway service road, close to where the previous couple had stopped. He saw what he believed to be a 1972 yellow VW Beetle with a black strip above its running board, affixed with what Spagnola thought were New York license plates. Another couple, Mr. and Mrs. Frank Vignoti, were parked in a car a short distance east of the park's entrance. While talking, they watched a man walk off the parkway overpass, coming from the area of the Graves End Bay esplanade. He walked in front of the Vignotis and crossed the service road to the yellow VW. He approached the driver's door and stopped as if to open it. At this point, he noticed the Vignotis looking at him and decided to continue on and enter the playground instead. He was white, stocky, short, about 5 ft 7 inches, with dark, short-cropped hair. He was dressed in dungarees and a white shirt which was tucked into his pants. His long sleeves were rolled up and his tan arms were well-defined and muscular.

Tommy Zaino was seated in a borrowed blue Corvette with his date. They were parked adjacent to the fence opposite the playground, just a short distance ahead of where the Vignotis were parked earlier. Zaino was parked directly under the sodium streetlamp near the overpass but had pulled forward two car lengths to park in a darker spot. At about 1:45 A.M., Zaino heard the distinctive sound of a VW engine and noticed a yellow VW roll by him on the one-way service road. A few minutes later, Robert Violante and Stacy Moskowitz pulled into the well-lit space recently vacated by Zaino. With the illumination from the streetlight and the added effect of the full moon, the Shore Parkway service road was almost as bright as day.

At the same time all of this was occurring, NYPD officer, Michael Cataneo, and his partner, Jeffrey Logan, drove onto Bay 17th Street, a quiet one-way avenue known for garden apartment buildings. The police spotted a cream-colored Ford Galaxy with a black vinyl roof, parked slightly behind a fire hydrant in front of number 290 Bay 17th Street. Berkowitz, in a courtyard between the apartment buildings, watched as Cataneo walked over to read the address on the wall of 290 Bay 17th Street and then returned to the curb to begin writing the ticket. He inscribed a 2:05 A.M. time designation on it, and then inserted the ticket behind the Galaxy's windshield wipers. The police car left only to stop again to ticket two double-parked autos further up the street near 262 Bay 17th Street.

Based on Maury Terry's investigation and interviews with Berkowitz, the following scenario was played out. Berkowitz saw the police about to ticket his car and reacted swiftly. In one of the most startling, significant, and ironic moments in the entire Son of Sam story, he decided to stop the planned shooting from occurring out of fear of the police being able to identify his car. He hurried back to the park and confronted at least two accomplices, telling them his car was at that moment being ticketed and that the attack should be cancelled or moved to another location. Berkowitz explained that the traceable ticket would make him vulnerable to arrest. An animated discussion ensued which Berkowitz lost. The alleged reasons to not put off the evening's attack purportedly involved plans that were in effect for that specific night, ones that could not easily be changed. Berkowitz was told to return to Bay 17th Street and to make sure that the police were clear of the area. He left the park at 2:10 A.M.

At 2:20 A.M., Cecilia Davis returned home after a night out with her friend, Howard Bohan. As they were saying their goodbyes for the evening, their car was double-parked and was blocking the street, so she kept her eye on the road behind them to make sure no cars were approaching. As she did so, she saw a young man emerge from the courtyard and lean across the Ford Galaxy's windshield and angrily remove a parking ticket. The man opened the driver's side door and then leaned against the ajar door and watched intently as the two police offers were issuing the second and third tickets. Davis observed the young man enter the Galaxy and speed up behind her and Howard. Clearly agitated, he blared his horn loudly. At this point, Davis climbed out of Howard's car. Standing on the curb, she looked at the profile of the impatient young man in the Galaxy as he passed. She noticed he was wearing a denim jacket and had dark, short-cropped hair. The Galaxy followed both Howard and the police across the Cropsey Avenue intersection. The Ford continued to the next intersection, Bay 17th and Bath Avenue, where it made a right turn. The Galaxy continued on, heading many blocks north and east of the Violante auto and the park. At this point, it was approximately 2:21 A.M., just 14 minutes before the shooting would occur.

At about the same time the Galaxy was leaving the area, two blocks away, Robert Violante and Stacy Moskowitz strolled into the park through the Shore Parkway entrance. Stacy and Robert, after arriving at the lover's lane at about 1:45 A.M., talked in the car for about twenty minutes before walking across the footbridge toward Graves End Bay. Upon returning to the park, they walked a path that separates a ball field and handball courts on the east side from the swings and bocce courts on the west side.

Leaning against a restroom building, in the shadows beneath a broken park light, near the end of the path, was a man Violante termed a "weird, grubby-looking hippie." His hair was dark, curly, and "all messed up, down over his forehead." He was stocky and wearing a blue-ish denim shirt or jacket with a tee-shirt underneath. His sleeves were rolled up. He was unshaven, tanned, and had piercing dark eyes. Robert and Stacy passed within ten feet of the man, who continued to lean against the restroom building as the couple entered the area where the swings were located. They returned to their car around 2:20 A.M. They did not see the man as they left. Zaino and another couple agreed with Violante's estimate of the time.

At approximately 2:23 A.M., Davis led her dog, Snowball, down the west side of Bay 17th Street and noticed the vacated space at the hydrant where the ticketed Galaxy was parked before. Looking at the service road, she saw three occupied cars, Violante's, Zaino's and a third auto, a VW bus. The time was approximately 2:30 A.M. Then, she and her dog walked back to the front of her apartment. A re-creation of these events would later show the entire trip took a minimum of 10 minutes. Davis gave into her pet's wishes, turned and retraced her steps towards Shore Parkway, but about 125 feet from her apartment she saw a young man "leaping the curb" to the sidewalk on her side of the block. He appeared to be coming from the other side of the street, the side away from the park. The man, who Davis later positively identified as David Berkowitz, and whose auto was also positively identified by the parking ticket, was just returning to the neighborhood after spending some time following the police officer that gave him the ticket.

He had been away from the area for a total of 13 minutes, and away from the park for 20 minutes. This information is crucial. As he walked by, less than 5 feet separated him from Davis. He was wearing a dark blue denim jacket with the sleeves rolled down. He had a shiny, grey-colored shirt on which was tucked into his denim trousers. She described his stomach as "large" and he was wearing what seemed to be blue deck shoes. His hair was short, dark, curly, and neatly combed. Berkowitz's right arm was held stiffly at his side as he turned to enter the courtyard and Mrs. Davis saw something she described as metallic, partially hidden up his right jacket sleeve. Berkowitz glared at her and, knowing he was not a neighborhood resident, she became a little frightened. Something seemed wrong with this man. She hurried to her first-floor apartment which was more than a two-block walk from the Violante auto. Upon arriving home, she immediately unleashed her dog and then opened a newspaper. At that moment, she heard a loud boom and a car horn blaring in the distance.

While Mrs. Davis was entering her apartment, Tommy Zaino, who was parked two car lengths in front of Violante's car on Shore Parkway, saw a man standing by a bench near the park's entrance. Zaino got a very good look at the man who was stationary, looking at Violante's car. He appeared to be 25-30 years of age, short, and stocky, with long, straight, messy, blondish hair, which was covering his forehead and part of his ears. "It looked like a wig," Zaino would say later. The man was wearing a grey-ish uniform-type shirt with long sleeves. The sleeves were rolled up to his elbows. The shirt was out of his trousers and he appeared to be unshaven. Zaino, who'd been looking out the Corvette's passenger window, now shifted his gaze to the rearview mirror as the man peered up and down the street and crossed the pavement while he approached the Violante auto.

Stacy and Robert were making out and oblivious to the menace approaching them. The blond-ish-haired man stopped about two feet from the car, pulled a gun from beneath his shirt, crouched, and fired 4 times through the open passenger window. Zaino, who was watching the entire incident frozen in place, later said he saw the gunman's hands "go up and down" between the shots. The attacker stopped firing, turned abruptly, and "runs like hell" into the darkened park and disappears. Zaino stated that he's never seen anyone run that fast. About a hundred yards away, on the opposite side of the park, at the 17th Avenue exit, a witness saw a white male, with dark eyebrows, possibly wearing a denim jacket, and wearing a light-colored cheap nylon wig, exit the park at a fast pace. He entered a small, light-colored auto and sped away. "He looks like he just robbed a bank," the witness stated. Concentrating on the license plate, she wrote down as much as she could discern. She thinks it either ends with "4-gur" or –"4-gvr." She wasn't able to read the first two numbers. At the same time, a 17th Avenue resident saw a car, whose make she couldn't identify, pull away from the park 20 seconds after the shots were fired. Likewise, a visiting nurse tending to a patient on 17th Avenue, also heard the shots and looked out her window only to see a yellow VW speeding north on 17th Avenue away from the park. She too, recorded a partial plate number, 463 but was unable to read the letters that follow.

At the corner of 17th Avenue and Cropsey Avenue, the yellow VW sped away through a red light with its lights out and the driver's left arm hanging out the window, as he struggled to hold the hastily-closed door shut. As the car careened through the light, it nearly collided with a car being driven by another witness, Alan Masters. Both autos came to a screeching halt in the center of the intersection. The VW driver leaned out his window and screamed "Motherfucker!" at the astonished Masters, then straightened out the car and roared west on Cropsey. Infuriated, Masters swung a sharp

U-turn and took off in pursuit. The VW driver, not realizing he was being chased, now turned on his headlights, but he quickly extinguished them when he spotted Masters bearing down on him. Masters, in a vain attempt to read the VW's license plate, hit the floor button for his high beams. He thought the plate may be a tan NJ plate, lighter than NY's amber, but he wasn't sure. The chase continued and at the end of Independence Avenue, the VW swerved to the right onto Bay 8 Street.

The driver then swung a hard U-turn all in one motion and headed straight back at Masters. The VW passed the witness and hurdled up the access ramp to the Belt Parkway. Masters, in pursuit, was blocked at the ramp's entrance by another car leaving the Parkway. Seconds later, he sped up the ramp, which offers entrances to the Belt in both East and West directions. He saw no taillights on the Eastbound lane, so he took the Westbound toward the Verrazano Narrows Bridge. By the time he reached 4th Street, he realized the VW had escaped. Masters was certain about the description of the VW's driver. He was male, white, 28-32 years old, with high cheek bones, face narrow at the bottom, a slight cleft in the chin, a flattish nose, with a shadowy, unshaven face, narrow-ish very dark eyes, hair messy, stringy, and brown combed from the left to the right. The VW driver was also wearing a bluish-gray long-sleeve shirt with the sleeves rolled up to the elbows.

Another witness observed yet another car leaving the scene in a highly suspicious manner. She was standing in front of her home on Bay 14th Street, shortly after the shots were fired, when she saw a small yellow car with its headlights flashing on and off as it sped past her. The headlight flashing technique is usually used when one wishes to prevent one's license plate numbers from being read. The lights are turned on to enable to driver to appraise the road ahead before turning them off again.

As the gunman disappeared into the dark, Robert Violante knew he was hurt badly. He heard Stacy moaning but he couldn't see her. A .44 bullet which smashed through his left eye and severely damaged the right one, had blinded him. Violante leaned long and hard on the Skylark's horn. He then stopped, climbed from the car, and wrapping one arm around the streetlamp, began to cry for help and pressed the horn again.

Tommy Zaino, who had witnessed the shooting, yelled out, "That was the fucking Son of Sam!" Zaino started the car up and drove as fast as he could to the 62nd precinct on Bath Avenue. After telling a cop standing on a corner by the station house about the shooting, he headed back to the scene. When Zaino arrived on Shore Road, Violante was lying on the street, an off-duty Port Authority Officer, Richard Sheehan, was standing over him. Together, they covered Violante with a blanket they found in the back of the victim's car. Stacy, gravely wounded, but still conscious, was sprawled across the Skylark's front seat. A few minutes later, officers Cataneo and Logan pulled up to the shooting scene. Cataneo looked into the car and saw Stacy. She didn't know she had been shot in the head and said to him, "I just got sick in the car."

It appeared that the Son of Sam outwitted the hapless Omega dragnet and struck in Brooklyn. He was the devil playing God and the NYPD seemed powerless to stop him. Police Commissioner Michael Codd acknowledged that the force's blanketing of Queens and the Bronx was a disastrous failure saying, "We've got an entire city to protect now. Sam is telling us he can strike anywhere."

The description of the yellow VW driver provided by Alan Masters would dovetail perfectly with Tommy Zaino's portrayal of the gunman, right down to the unshaven face and rolled up sleeves. It was also very similar to Violante's description of the "grubby looking hippie" in the park. And with the exception of the hair, it matched the description the Vignottis would supply of the man who approached the yellow VW on the service road an hour before the shooting. But in no way whatsoever would the descriptions provided by Masters, Zaino, Violante or the Vignottis match Mrs. Davis' account of the man who would turn out to be David Berkowitz. When one takes into account all of the information and witness statements involving this crime, it's impossible to imagine that Berkowitz was the shooter.

In addition to the descriptions given by various witnesses, the timeline does not allow for Berkowitz to be the shooter on Shore Parkway. Mrs. Davis put David Berkowitz totally out of the area beginning at 2:20 A.M. when she saw him leave to follow the police who had just ticketed his car. He was still away from the park at 2:33 A.M., just two minutes before the attack, when he passed Mrs. Davis on foot while she was walking the dog.

Several years after the shooting, Maury Terry had Mrs. Davis recreate her walk with the dog. Based on the time the ticket was issued and placed on the Galaxy, the sighting by three witnesses of the shooter leaning against the park building, and Mrs. Davis' sightings of David Berkowitz taking the ticket off the Galaxy, and then again when he passed her, proves without a shadow of a doubt that Berkowitz couldn't be the shooter.

The Brooklyn scenario had a beginning, the 2:05 A.M. ticket, and ended with the attack at 2:35 A.M. With those bookends, Howard Bohan's watch, numerous interviews, and the timings of the movements of the principles and measurement of the distances travelled, this final recreation of the last two minutes was accurate. This too, was a step the police never took.

Howard Bohan was never interviewed by police.

According to David Berkowitz, the Moskowitz/Violante shooting was filmed, which had to be the reason the others didn't allow him to call it off. According to Maury, the red VW van that was seen by witnesses near the park house contained three occupants: Ron Sisman, the cameraman; and two others whom Maury identified by pseudonyms.

It is alleged that Roy Radin was involved because he approached Robert Mapplethorpe to make a snuff film. As per Jesse Turner, Robert Mapplethorpe approached Ronald Sisman to carry out the request.

The noted occult author, Peter Levenda, stated that Roy Radin approached him back in the mid-1970s and asked if Levenda could set up some filming of satanic rituals. Levenda did not assist Radin, but it is interesting that Radin is now known for asking for help in setting up and filming satanic rituals as well as the Brooklyn shooting.

Some of the information presented in this chapter seems a bit outlandish, but I ask you, is it more believable than Berkowitz acting on his own at the behest of his talking dog? I think we all know the answer to that.

Ten

In 1993, Maury Terry was able to procure a jailhouse interview with David Berkowitz. At that point, the rumours of Berkowitz not acting alone when it came to the Son of Sam murders were pretty much dead in the water. Although they were still well known to many people across America, there hadn't been any new developments in years. But it seemed that while in prison Berkowitz had become a born-again Christian and there were some things that he wanted to get off his chest. Maury was ready to listen.

While Maury had received a lot of information over the years from prison informants, it was nothing compared to being able to interview Berkowitz himself and getting his take on what happened. This could be a game changer.

When Maury first reached out to Berkowitz to see if he was game for the interview, Berkowitz said, "It's been a very long time. I'm prepared to talk about some of the main parts of the case, but I can't talk about all of it or about any of these people who are still alive."

That was okay by Maury, or at least he told Berkowitz that. Maury got the interview and it was broadcast on *Inside Edition* to much fanfare.

Berkowitz told Maury he joined the cult in 1975. He was initiated by Michael Carr after he met him at a party in the Bronx. "I was lonely, looking for friends, and I'd always been intrigued by the occult," he recalled. "They presented all this to me in a harmless way—just witchcraft and seances and so forth. Plus, there were a few attractive girls in it. I had no idea what was in store. I never dreamed I'd eventually become a murderer."

Berkowitz said the cult members met up regularly at parties and bars and would also occasionally meet up at local beaches and parks. He later realized he was being groomed to be a bigger part of the cult. He said at that point there were a few less than two dozen people in the group, hence the name 22 Disciples of Hell.

He said of this time, "I didn't realize it then, but now I can see that I was being brought along slowly. In time, they took me to Untermeyer."

Things at Untermeyer got pretty strange fast. "I was initiated at Untermeyer," he told Maury. "I recited a prayer to Lucifer and then pricked my finger to draw a little blood. I also gave information about my family, which was stupid of me to do. After that, the whole thing got more serious. There were animal sacrifices and some small arsons in Yonkers and the Bronx. There was also drug dealing and some illegal weapons around."

He went on. "Shortly after that, I was told to move to Pine Street. Things were heating up, and the center of activity had shifted to that part of Yonkers, and they wanted me nearby."

Berkowitz told Maury his version of what went down during each attack. When it came to Donna Lauria, he said, "I did shoot Donna, and I'm very sorry about doing it. She was known by some in the group, and so it actually wasn't random, although the public believed it was." He later added it was "very possible" Donna and her girlfriend Jody Valente were "followed that entire evening." He also said three other accomplices were at the scene, including Michael Carr. "I was with Michael," Berkowitz said. "The other two were in a tan car."

He said of my shooting, "A woman shot him (meaning me). There were several of us there that night," Berkowitz said, adding that three of those "several" conspirators were women. The shooter is believed to be one of two prime suspects, Wendy or Amy.

When it came to the shootings of Joanne Lomino and Donna DeMasi, he simply said, "That was John Carr."

He was more talkative when it came to Christine Freund. "I believe there was a motive to this, but I don't know what it was." Berkowitz told Maury "at least five" conspirators were present that night. "It was different because they brought someone in from out of town to do it," he said of the killer. Berkowitz let out that "Manson II" was the shooter. He added, "There was another guy with him when he came to New York, and that person was also out there that night," and, "They did use a red car in this shooting."

When it came to the Virginia Voskerichian shooting he told Maury, "A woman from Westchester did it. I was there, too, but it was her who wore that watch cap. The Brooklyn shooting was another that was a woman—and the third was Mike Carr. I was aware Sam Carr went to the authorities and so forth, so I knew they'd be coming very soon. It's not hard to see how I knew this— and so everything was arranged."

Berkowitz explained the reason he confessed to the killings. "I did do two of the shootings—that's three deaths— and I played a role in the rest. So what's the difference if I said I did all of them? I knew I was going to jail for life no matter what, and I deserved to. Plus, I was sticking loyal to the others in the group."

Berkowitz also said that once he visited the group's headquarters in White Plains in 1976. "They had a big role in all of it." He also said there were numerous members of the Process Church at the house. "They tossed different ideas around," Berkowitz said. "One of them was to kidnap young girls and kill them in cemeteries. Another was to copy the Manson thing in rich neighbourhoods. But the goal was to paralyze New York, and they eventually decided on the .44 shootings."

Maury asked if they were ever involved in the Manson killings and Berkowitz said yes. "The Process was very sophisticated and dedicated," Berkowitz told Maury. "They had their hands in a lot of things, including drugs and that disgusting child pornography. They also provided kids for sex to some wealthy people, and I did see some of those people at parties."

One might think that the words of Berkowitz pointing the finger at other shooters would have changed everything, but after a brief furor, things died back down again.

Berkowitz sang pretty much the same tune in a 1999 interview with Larry King. The following is part of the transcript from that interview.

> *King: By the way, did you always act alone?*
>
> *Berkowitz: Well, not really. Not totally like that.*
>
> *King: Were other people caught?*
>
> *Berkowitz: No. I just felt I had no mind. I just felt something else was controlling, controlling me...*
>
> *King: And you took it through a dog?*
>
> *Berkowitz No, no, that was...*
>
> *King: What was that?*
>
> *Berkowitz: That was just -- I'd rather not talk about that. That was just a bunch of...*
>
> *King: I'm not going to pressure you, but there were pressures on you.*
>
> *Berkowitz: Yes, sure, there were pressures.*
>
> *King: You were hearing from sources outside of yourself?*
>
> *Berkowitz: Not in that psychological way, but it was a satanic thing. It was..*
>
> *King: They're still out there?*

Berkowitz: Most have passed on. And—

King: But they were involved in killing as well?

Berkowitz: They were—

King: They got away with it?

Berkowitz: Well, no, they haven't gotten away with it, and they won't.

Or will they? Let's face it, the police had their man, and the case was closed. Not only that, but Berkowitz was thought of as a lunatic, largely because of the talking dog. The police weren't going to anything without absolute proof.

When writing this book, it occurred to me, that maybe, just maybe, Berkowitz might open up to me and tell the total truth about who shot me. He didn't know I was writing a book, as far as he knew I was just a victim looking for closure. And if I lied to him a little bit to get the information about who put a bullet in my head, so what? It wasn't like I owed him anything. At the very least, he was involved in my shooting and numerous other deaths. It wasn't like I was going to feel bad misleading him.

Not only that, but Berkowitz was supposedly a changed man. As he writes on his website that he runs from prison, *"As I have communicated many times throughout the years, I am deeply sorry for the pain, suffering and sorrow I have brought upon the victims of my crimes. I grieve for those who are wounded, and for the family members of those who lost a loved one because of my selfish actions. I regret what I've done and I'm haunted by it.*

Not a day goes by that I do not think about the suffering I have brought to so many. Likewise I cannot even comprehend all the grief and pain they live with now. And these individuals have every right to be angry with me, too.

Nevertheless, I apologize for the crimes I committed. My continual prayer is that, as much as is possible, these hurting individuals can go on with their lives.

In addition, I am not writing this apology for pity or sympathy. I simply believe that such an apology is the right thing to do. And, by the grace of God, I hope to do my very best to make amends whenever and wherever possible, both to society, and to my victims.

Okay, so apparently he feels bad about my suffering. Maybe he would do something about it and give me some details. As far as I know, Berkowitz has never communicated with any of his surviving victims, so I decided to write him and see if we get a little honest conversation going.

I wrote him a letter through JPay, which is a way to send electronic communication to prisoners. The Tracy Ann I mention in the letter is a woman who was "saved" by Berkowitz through his online ministry. This is what it said.

Hi David,

I hope this letter finds you in good health. How are your new digs at Wallkill? Funny, that is the same name as my Dad's fire house. My dad passed away a few years ago, and a day doesn't go by that I don't miss him. I think you came in contact with his church in Circleville 15 years ago. I believe some of the congregation was doing bible studies with you at Sullivan.

The reason I'm writing you today is to see if you would be willing to meet with me. My 44th anniversary of being shot is coming up and I would love to have some closure. I know you didn't shoot me and I'm pretty sure I know who did. I would love to talk with you and get the answers I have been looking for the past 30 years. I realize there is very little upside for you to tell all and spend the rest of your time in protective custody. I will not pressure you to go into details but hope springs eternal and I figured I would put it out there for you to ponder. At the very least I think it would be cathartic for both of us to meet, pray and talk, even if we just talk about life, forgiveness and maybe Maury!

Your friend, Tracy Anne had contacted me to tell me her story. I responded and she mentioned that you wanted to meet with me. I have to tell you, I have been waiting for a sign to contact you and I think Tracy Anne gave it to me. I am a practicing catholic and a 3rd degree Knight of Columbus, and I know how powerful prayer can be.

I would love to sit down and talk and pray with you, man to man and put this ugly piece of history behind us both. David, is all I›m looking for is closure. I know you didn›t shoot me and you are truly sorry for the pain caused by some bad decisions. I am hoping that both our souls will be cleansed and we can move on. Meeting with you could be a cathartic experience for both of us. Please write me as soon as you are able. Looking forward to hearing from you.

Stay well.

Carl Denaro

It was pretty odd writing a letter to the guy who supposedly had shot me in the head decades ago, but it was something I had wanted to do for a long time. I had no idea whether he would write me back or not, but it didn't take too long before I heard back. While he talked a good game, he certainly wasn't being all that up-front with me about anything.

His letter read:

Dear Carl,

I received your letter which I downloaded from the community kiosk just yesterday. Hearing from you is surreal. I never thought the day would come. Thank you, I wanted to reach out, if this is even the best way to say it "reach out" to you and the other victims and their families for the longest. Prison rules prohibit this. I am not permitted to contact you on my own. Thus your email is an answer to my prayers.

But anyway I want to let you know that I am beyond words to hear from you. I want to take some time to absorb everything.

I am sorry to learn of your dads passing. Yes, years ago there was someone from your dad's church whom I ran into. I don't remember who it was. But as a Christian I can see how God has his hands upon our lives, even now, and even by allowing us to correspond.

I hope to answer you. Letter soon. I pray you are well. I also pray for your continued healing. I cannot even begin to imagine the pain and suffering you've had to endure.

I am so very sorry.

I've already let Tracey know that I have heard from you. God Bless you Carl. I will write again soon.

Sincerely, David.

Psalm 23

Okay, so that was cool, I mean I guess it was. He said all sorts of nice things, but he really gave me nothing. And to be honest, does it really matter if someone who shot you in the head for no reason at all says nice things about it?

I decided to try again and ramp it up a little.

Hi David,

All good on my end. How are you doing? I guess I wasn't clear as to why I wrote you back on August 13Th. I read your letter on Arise and Shine website, talking about the SOS shows that keep being made. I just wanted to let you know I go through the same thing. You know, they interview you for 2 hours and when the interview airs it doesn't resemble the interview at all. Basically they use my voice to put out the story they want to put out. True or false, they don't really care.

You got me thinking about what you have experienced in the last 45 years. Specifically, the technology. Never really thought about that. Making a call on a cell phone, PC's, tablets, email, etc. The electric bikes, motorized skateboards to name a few new modes of transportation. Hard for me to wrap my head around that whole concept of watching the world go by.

I speak with Maury's ex-wife Georgiana fairly regularly. I know she writes you via snail mail. She is a very nice person. With a few health problems. I actually met her at Maury's wake. We hung for about 7 hours and became fast friends. Keep praying for Gi. I do every day.

Maury...He was an enigma. I considered him a friend, mentor, hero and a musical encyclopedia. We spent many hours on the phone and would meet once a month at his favorite New York City watering hole, Kennedy's. But as much as I enjoyed his company and intelligence he had another side that wasn't that pretty! Maury's way or no way! I used to kid him about his huge ego and asked him how his back could handle carrying it around.

I just spoke with Josh Zeman, Maury's hand-picked biographer and documentarian. I know he said he was going to talk with you but I don't know if he ever got around to it.

I hope you and I can actually meet someday. I'm assuming that in person visits have been stopped for the time being due to the Covid virus. How do you handle that? Do they give you mask masks, gloves and sanitizer? I hope so. If you need any of that and they aren't providing it, let me know. I will send you what you need.

Let me know if you want to talk to me about my experience, or any other aspect of that terrible time. Like I said in my first letter, I just want some kind of closure. Hoping you can help me with that.

I'll close for now. I hope to hear from you soon. Stay safe.

Peace,
Carl

His second letter was more of the same.

Hi Carl!

Hope all with you. I wish for you Gods peace health safety and favor. I wish and pray the same for your family. I have your email dated Aug 13. The way it begins I cannot be sure if you received my first email. They system is still new and there has been glitches. Sometimes an email will not get sent. This included emails coming in and out. Otherwise it is a blessing to have the privilege of electronic mail, I've had to reply on snail mail for more than 40 years now. But sometimes it has its advantages

Technology has advanced to the extent that I feel as if I've been left behind. We were first issued our tablets in October of last year. I remember being intimidated by it. I've never even used a cell phone. This is a different world than the one I remember.

The city is different as well. Gone are the subway and bus tokens. And so much more. In certain ways I am stuck in the past and cannot imagine what life outside is like now.

Maury was a good man and I miss him. He died an outcast to the powers that be, media, local government and even law enforcement. I regret not getting to know him better.

I have enormous pain and grief and regret over what happened those 40 plus years ago. I think I may have mentioned this in my previous email, but by God's Grace I try to move forward. An endless stream of Son of Sam crime shows doesn't make it easier, that is for sure but such is life. I certainly can't even begin to imagine what you've had to go through. However, I am so very sorry. Feel free to write whenever you wish.

I wrote him once more, asking once again for some form of closure, but Berkowitz continued to be vague and beat around the bush when he replied, writing:

Hi Carl,

I have your email of 9/2, it still seems surreal to me that we're corresponding. I believe in miracles and this is truly one of them.

The kiosk device that we have here allows for me to send out and receive emails. It's been less than a year that I have been able to get a tablet device. I'm still learning the ropes. Prior to email I had to resort to snail mail which I still use. But having email is a real blessing. I believe God made this possible by moving the hearts of prison officials to allow for this kind of exchange.

And I also believe that God had it in mind that through this kind of communication which had to do without for over 40 years you and I would be able to talk and share our thoughts. And for both of us it will, I hope, bring about healing and a degree of closure.

As for me, the Jewish high holy day, which many Jews consider to be one of the most sacred days of the year, Rosh Hashanah, represents not only the entrance into another year, but the opportunity for a new beginning. According to the Jewish beliefs this is a time which calls for confession of ones sins and seeking forgiveness for them and for wiping the slate clean so to speak, thus allowing for a fresh start. I have to leave now. I hope to continue this letter shortly. Have much to share. Thank you Carl for giving me the chance to make things right. Some events from the past could never be undone but some can.

One of my favorite verses in the Psalms says as follows "The Lord is gracious and full of compassion, slow to anger and of great mercy.

Be Well, David

Enough already. It was becoming apparent I wasn't going to get what I was looking for unless I became more aggressive. I decided to stop dancing around and ask him some straight-out questions. I figured if I did so I would either scare him away, or I would get my questions answered about who shot me once and for all. My letter is as follows.

Hi David,

Hope this email finds you well. I guess this COVID pandemic is not going away to quickly. I hope the prison officials are doing the right thing and protecting everybody from this horrible virus. Life has changed dramatically for all of us in the last 6 months and it appears we will never get back to normal. Oh well, better to be safe and quarantined as the alternative is not that good either!

I am hoping you will be willing to share a few thoughts from the past with me. As I have stated several times, I am just looking for closure. With Rosh Hashanah just behind us, I thought this would be a good time to start this dialogue.

Was I targeted to be a victim?

Who made that decision?

You told Maury on national TV that you didn't shoot me but you know a woman shot me. Maury had given me both of the following names.

Was it a woman named Amy?

Was it Wheat Carr?

Who was your friend and accomplice "Richie?" Maury told me that he passed away but never told me his real identity.

Were you friends with a person Maury identified as Gorman. Johnson?

Was he at any of the shootings? Can you verify what was the name of the real Gorman Johnson.

I can only assume these are tough questions for you to answer but I need to know the truth. Too many lies, untruths and made up stories have plagued this case since the beginning. Now is the time to get the truth out.

I am confident you will do your best to help bring closure to this dark episode of both of our lives.

Please, let's start with these few questions and see where we go from there.

Thanks in advance for your help and cooperation.

Once this COVID thing ends I would love to come visit you.

Keep the faith. Stay safe and take care of yourself.

Sincerely,

Carl Denaro

I felt like I truly accomplished something after I sent that letter, knowing there was no way he was going to weasel out of answering those questions, but then weeks went by and I heard nothing back. I knew he was thinking about telling the truth to me, or at least paying lip service to it. Below is a post from his website that he keeps active from prison that he wrote around the same time my letters were arriving.

Throughout the past forty years my life has been molded and shaped by the whims of the entertainment industry. I've heard the most absurd and ridiculous ideas and theories espoused as to why the crime spree happened, along with tales of my life that were untrue and inaccurate.

As I wrote in a recent entry, such private speculations by these "experts," if they were voiced in a courtroom setting, could be challenged. They would be compelled to explain how they arrived at their conclusions, and I believe their "professional" views would be shattered.

I grieve all the misinformation that gets put on the public. I hope and pray for the chance to share the true story of who David Berkowitz is, and the real factors behind the Son of Sam case.

At first, I was kind of pissed off he didn't write me back, then I thought it was possible that prison officials read my letter to him and didn't send it along. Maybe its sensitive nature was against the rules. So, I wrote him one more time and tried to be a bit more sensitive.

Hi David,

Hope this email finds you well.

Did you get my letter from October 9? I haven't heard back from you and wanted to make sure all is good. I asked you a few questions and wasn't sure if the officials blocked the letter or you just haven't responded.

I am hoping you will be willing to share a few thoughts from the past with me. As I have stated several times, I am just looking for closure. I would love to hear your answers to my original questions.

Below is a shortened version of the questions I asked you 3 weeks ago. Please respond one way or another.

Was I targeted?

Who made that decision?

You stated on national TV that you didn't shoot me, a woman shot me.

Who was it?

Were the Dorfler's at the house on 156th street?

"Richie's" last name? he died some time ago

Thanks in advance for your help and cooperation. Once this COVID quarantine ends I would like to come visit you.

Keep the faith. Stay safe and take care of yourself.

Peace.

Carl Denaro

Just when I figured I had lost him for good, he wrote back, and this time he came closer than ever to giving me the information I sought.

His letter, dated November 1, 2020, is as follows.

Dear Carl,

I hope this letter finds you doing well and healthy. I continue to pray for you and wish you the very best. I received your email dated October 9 as well as two other more recent letters. I apologize for the slow response. I've been meaning to write and had every intention to do so. But

I am a chronic procrastinator and always fall behind with many things. Sorry. The things you asked me about are very painful for me. I have consulted an attorney about these issues and have been awaiting his reply. And as you may already know, all our emails are routinely recorded and filed away. They are always subject to review by law enforcement. The same with phone calls.

This fact is always given to me whenever I use the telephone or kiosk to send out my emails. Not that you and I are discussing anything illegal, God forbid. But even discussing legal related issues can easily be misconstrued, especially in older criminal cases. So I always have to be aware of my surroundings. I guess my years of incarceration and having to survive in prison has made me more aware of potential problems and misunderstandings than the average individual. As I shared before Maury and I had our ups and downs. I miss him. His unfortunate sickness slowed down the progress he was making followed by his untimely death. He and I started our communications shortly after my arrest. Then the Carr brothers died soon after. Many sad outcomes to include the unexpected passing of Craig Glassman. Haunting and frightening.

But I must end this now. Please be patient.
My best to you,
David.

I have to admit this raised my hopes. Could it be, after all these years I would finally find out the truth? I was shot in the head by a total stranger for no reason at all in one of the most famous criminal cases in America's history. Would I finally find out the truth?

I gave it a few days so as not to appear too eager, then wrote back.

Hi David,

Hope all is well. I understand about procrastinating! I too am a chronic procrastinator. The silver lining is that I seem to do my best work when I have a deadline. My work as a telecommunications auditor fits in perfectly with procrastination flaw. I must report my findings to my clients at a regularly scheduled meeting, so I know exactly when I need to have my work completed.

I understand the questions I asked you must be very painful, but I know that you already told Maury most of what I asked you. As I said in my earlier letters to you, Maury told me a lot a things but he kept a lot of his knowledge to himself. Now that he is no longer with us, I have no one else to turn to for the answers I am searching for.

I am aware that the prison officials monitor all your correspondence and I assumed that law enforcement has access to that same information if they chose to look at it. I don't think law enforcement has any desire to investigate any of this. They still hold on to you as the lone gunman, taking orders from a dog.

I am curious to know what your lawyer has told you regarding talking about the case. I am not a lawyer, but I can't see any legal reasons that would prohibit you or me to discuss the case. You have stated many times that you are sick and tired of people making up stories about you and the case. We all know other people were involved and you were the fall guy. Most of the people involved are dead and I know that some are still alive and living their lives out in freedom.

I also realize that your personal safety could be in jeopardy by revealing names and discussing the case. I too, have the same issues. I have continued to investigate this case and worry about the consequences. But, I have come to the conclusion that at this late stage people would be more likely to ignore allegations and deny everything as opposed to retaliating.

Yes, Maury was making progress and his untimely death ended all that. I am hoping that I can pick up that mantle and continue on. You mentioned the untimely death of Craig Glassman. Haunting and frightening. Can you elaborate on that? I know he was killed in an automobile accident on Halloween but don't know much more.

I hope you can answer some of my questions and we continue to communicate with each other. Hopefully some day we can meet face to face..

Stay safe, stay well.

Peace,

Carl Denaro

As of this writing it's been about 6 weeks since I wrote that letter to Berkowitz. I haven't heard back.

Eleven

As the years went by, Maury and I not only continued working on investigating the case together, but we also stayed close friends. Sometimes we would talk for hours on the phone, as much as three times a week. Whenever we spoke, I asked him about his health. I knew he wasn't doing that great in that area and I worried about him. I would also ask about the updated version of the book and how he was progressing with it. He would always say he was getting there, that he was working on it. Then Maury always asked me about how I was doing with money and how my daughter was. This was standard until the day he died.

Finally, in 2010, Maury said he wasn't going to wait anymore to put the book out. He was going to update the book and let the chips fall where they may. The years had turned into decades and the case was still not fully solved. People were still walking around free who had gotten away with murder, and just as importantly to Maury, the truth had still yet to be known to the vast majority of people. This was Maury's life's work; it had to see the light of day.

I wanted Maury to put up a website as a place to sell his updated book. According to him, no publisher had the guts to handle it and all his old editions of *The Ultimate Evil* had gone out of print. Instead, he wanted to do a Facebook group to get the word out about the new version of the book. I didn't like this idea but when Maury got something in his head, it was hard to break him of it.

We started a page called The Official Maury Terry "The Ultimate Evil" Son of Sam and Beyond and started putting up a lot of information on Facebook. To the rest of the people in the group, it was exciting; but to me, I had known everything that he was posting for the past 10 years. It was good information, but it was nothing that was going to break the case open. If it was, it would have happened 10 years ago. The page was followed by law enforcement, Son of Sam aficionados, researchers, and the just plain curious.

One of the things he teased the Facebook group with when it came to fresh information was the true identity of the cult leader, also known as Mr. Real Estate. Maury had given me his identity back in 2006. Maury told me the identity of Mr. Real Estate. After Maury gave me the name of Mr. Real Estate, I then spent 9 years trying to connect the dots and prove without a shadow of a doubt his involvement in the murders. As hard as I tried, I never had been able to quite get there.

After Maury's death, the FB group started clamouring for the real name of Mr. Real Estate, saying if they had it, they could blow the whole case wide open. Obviously, if that were the case, it already would have happened. To Maury and to me, this case was solved many years ago. Maury knew who the leader of the cult was way back in the 90s and even alerted the police. Nothing came of it. He would have blown the case open back then if he could have but he kept running into brick walls. The police didn't have a lot of incentive to open the case back up, they had their man, and that was that.

The Facebook group continued to grow and Maury was in his glory. His childhood friend, Charles, and I were the administrators of the page, but this was Maury's baby all the way. Maury's personality traits were in full bloom, he was like a puppet master, pulling strings behind the scenes.

At his worst, Maury was secretive, controlling, and dominating. The Facebook group gave him full rein to exercise those traits. Maury fed Charles info and messages that he wanted posted, much of which was hard for most of the group members to figure out.

Here is a post that Maury put up, in theory to give people clues as to who Mr. Real Estate was. Even with knowing his name, the clues don't seem to match up to Donovan. Below is the actual post from the Facebook group.

THE OFFICIAL MAURY TERRY "THE ULTIMATE EVIL" - SON OF SAM & BEYOND GROUP

WHAT IS THIS?

Well for one thing, it is a new quiz....

This one even will be called "WHAT Is This?"

So...what is this – and why does it matter? Or does it?

Clues? Sure....

Connected to the overall SOS investigation.

Not exactly Polaroid, but kind of.

An Atlanta neighbourhood.

A Boston team.

Texas and Wyoming qualify.

A Ray Charles hit song – sort of.

Regarding a devilish plot.

White Christmas Sisters.

Untermeyer Park? Yes, it was.

A quote from a space alien?

What happened when the outlaw shot at Annie Oakley?

There you go. Easy, right?

This time, the fantastic prize will be a four day, one-way cruise from New York on the steamer "Juicy Lusi."

This fine ship is a direct descendant of the famed "Lusitania," which was torpedoed near the coast of Ireland by a German submarine 100 years ago this month. (See the first Comments Box.)

So, good luck to all, and now it is time for "All hands on deck!" - in a manner of speaking.

* * * * * * * *

RESULTS

Three people got the correct answer on their own. "Likes" do not count.

It was in fact "Mr. Real Estate's" funeral.

But as for actually deciphering the clues...doubtful.

Regardless, congrats to Al X, Eric Anderson, and Patrick Duffy.

They get to share a small stateroom with bunks on the "Lusitania II's" 2016 "Hot Summer" cruise through the tranquil Arabian Sea.

As you can see, this was about as clear as mud. Maury wasn't trying to give out information, he was trying to conceal it unless someone proved themselves worthy. This is the kind of thing Maury was always doing. Instead of just telling people something, he would make up some long, convoluted riddle to try and make them guess it. Oddly enough, the only other person I can think of that did such things was the writer of the Son of Sam letters.

Maury posted a lot of riddles. It's hard to tell if Maury's love for riddles came from reading the ones attributed to Berkowitz in his letters to Jimmy Breslin, or if he was fascinated with the letters because of his love for riddles.

Much like the Son of Sam supposedly loved teasing Breslin and the police, Maury loved teasing the group. He would often put up clues that were supposed to lead members to a name of someone involved with the attacks or to who an anonymous photo was of, but most of them were so obscure they were impossible to figure out. If people didn't guess enough at what the answer may be or act like they were interested, Maury would get very angry and go off on a rant about people not caring enough about the group. Maury would get so upset he would threaten to withhold info from them in the future. My daughter was a member of the group and Maury would even give me a hard time about her not hitting the "like" button enough.

An example of an easy riddle that he posted was:

A Beatle Once
Quaker
Beast of Burden
Gimme Shelter
Which came out to:
Best
Friends
Animal
Sanctuary

Best Friends Animal Sanctuary is an offshoot of The Process Church of Final Judgment. These riddles were just another way to keep the group on their toes as well as to mess with their minds.

The group grew quite rapidly over the first year, but Maury had us administrators kick out a bunch of people; some for being sympathizers with the Process Church of Final Judgement, and others because he considered them lurkers; in other words, those who didn't participate enough.

He continued to stress to me that this was our last chance to get the truth out there. He was going to redo the book, publish it, and name names, and by the time the people he named get around to suing him, he would be dead. We were going to name "Mr. Real Estate," the leader of the cult, as well as the convicted pedophile known as the "boss" of David Berkowitz.

We also were going to name some of the foot soldiers who did some of the shootings. We knew through an interview with Berkowitz that the person who shot me was a woman, and we were pretty sure we knew who it was. We also were certain, through years of investigation, that we knew who the triggerman was in the shootings of Stacy Moskowitz and Robert Violante.

In his mind, if he put the names of people involved out there and made people nervous and jammed up, maybe someone would have a conscience, maybe someone might even say something on their deathbed. Maury knew there would never be enough proof to solve the case unless Berkowitz talked and said something definitive or someone came forward and said they're part of the cult.

Another reason he was flummoxed about what to do with the information was he wasn't sure where to go with it. Would he bring it to his local precinct? The District Attorney? The FBI? Berkowitz doesn't talk because he doesn't have anyone he could trust. If he told the truth, the reality is the other people involved just would have kept going with the talking dog thing.

There were other parts of Maury's master plan. Once Maury finished the book and it came out, I would hire a lawyer and start a civil suit against NYC to get press. The NYPD wouldn't want the case reopened, but in a civil case, you can subpoena people which would rattle some cages and get more attention for the book.

Maury continued to talk to me about his "master plan" all the time. He would update the book, it would come out and garner attention, cages would be rattled, I would get some money from the NYPD because they did such an awful job and people might come out of the woodwork. We would get press and the case would be reopened.

When Kennedy's closed, we lost our mutual meeting place. During the same time period, Maury's health went downhill. Soon after the closing, Maury called me from the hospital informing me he had congestive heart failure. Luckily, he survived that scare and went home. Unbeknownst to me, this, unfortunately, was the beginning of the end for Maury. Although we continued to talk and email each other, I would never see Maury alive again. For the next four years, I invited him out to lunch, invited myself to visit him at his house, and tried to get him come see some live music at a watering hole close to where he lived, but to no avail. I didn't realize it at the time, but Maury had become a hermit. He said he had to get his teeth fixed, his hair cut, and do a hundred other things before he would go out in public. He confided in me that he had to carry around an oxygen machine. He didn't have to tell me this, but his ego would not allow him to go out in public with this "old person" contraption tethered to his body. I guess I always thought that this was a temporary thing until I got the word from his nephew that Maury had passed away.

I was in mourning for a long time. It felt like a piece of me was gone. I considered Maury a hero. Without Maury, I wouldn't even know that other people were involved in my shooting. It was him and him alone that brought this to my attention. We became friends within the first 5 minutes of meeting and then I became his protege. As the years went on, I almost became his peer. Often when he stumbled over a name or the details of some situation, I would correct him. He gave me advice and I trusted his judgment; I always took a back seat to Maury. Friend, mentor, hero. My hope was that with the new book I could have total closure on a traumatic event that happened 35 years ago.

The Facebook page is still active today after Maury's death, but it is a bit adrift. Between not knowing who is seeing posts, that this book is in the process of being written, and the fact we were all a bit under Maury's spell, it's hard to know what should be let out in the open and what still should be kept secret.

There was a woman that used to post on the page all the time named Trudy Leek. Her profile said she was from San Antonio, but it didn't have much info on it other than that. She was always very supportive of everything Maury had to say and was also very critical of many other posters.

She knew a lot about the case. So much that it was making me uncomfortable. She knew all sorts of facts that someone not seriously involved in the case shouldn't know, and, although in theory she was from San Antonio, she knew a ton about Yonkers. I started to investigate her, but I couldn't find out anything about her. I told Maury I didn't trust her. That there was no way she was who she was saying she was.

Maury assured me that she was cool, and that all was fine, but I didn't buy it. Three times I told Maury I thought Trudy was a fake account that he was using. He denied it each time, but after his death, I found out from one of the other administrators that it was true; Maury was Trudy. Just another example of him giving one person information while withholding it from someone else.

This was part of the dark side of Maury's personality. He could be controlling, secretive, and demanding. And he definitely got a kick out of playing games, just like the supposed Son of Sam did. Maury would often give me a piece of information that was totally different than what he would give to someone else. As much as it seemed that Maury wanted to know the whole truth about the Son of Sam murders, he was equally concerned with being in control of everything and being the only person that understood the whole picture.

Still, he did some amazing work. Some of *The Ultimate Evil* may have been exaggerated, but he should have won an award for the first three quarters of the book. Everything in that section is backed up with facts, although, in my opinion, he should have ended it 150 pages sooner. He legitimately proved that Berkowitz couldn't have done all the shootings. It was totally solid.

Once he got to the California part of the book, there was a lot of information that he put out there with very little evidence. Things to do with the Zodiac Killer and his connection with Manson. Much of it seemed like a cheap plug to gain interest in the book. No one buys into that part of the book. Because of that, he opened up the doors for everyone to call him a conspiracy theorist and mock him. As a person, Maury was a lot like his book *The Ultimate Evil.* Ninety-five percent of him was brilliant and true, but the rest of him was just a little bit larger than life.

After his death, his ex-wife, Georgianna, told me that he had sent her the unfinished updated book. She sent me a copy and I was very disappointed when I found that the information promised in this new edition was nowhere to be found. I was hoping that at least some of the pseudonyms that he used for the suspects would be revealed so I could continue my investigation into the case. Unfortunately, he continued to use the same pseudonyms for subjects in his updated version. After his death, I started contacting some of his friends that had helped in the investigation, and also some of the more reliable members of the Facebook group. What I found out while talking to these people was disheartening. Apparently, Maury, always the puppet master, doled out different snippets of information on the case to members of the inner circle. When we started comparing notes, it was clear to us that information was withheld to some of us but given to other members. In some cases, the information was actually misinformation. It seems that when some of the researchers came back with new information for Maury, he dismissed it and sent them in another direction. Of course, this made me feel sad, disgusted, and betrayed. It prompted me to ask more questions of more people, which led me to start questioning everything Maury had told me.

One example was what Maury revealed to me about who Mr. Real Estate was. He gave me his name and I spent ten years trying to get background on this suspect. When Maury gave ten clues identifying Mr. Real Estate to the Facebook group, his little quiz certainly spurred the members of the FB group on to investigate the identity of Mr. Real Estate. For me, knowing the real identity and the ten clues, I still couldn't find anything on the guy.

I took a back seat and took directions. He would give me a name and I would research it, but for the most part I didn't even know why. In retrospect, I wish I had questioned him more and not just followed blindly. But it was hard to doubt someone who had made this case his life's work.

When I realized Maury was fielding different and conflicting information to different people, I was angry that he deceived me and, in some cases, out and out lied to me.

It wasn't just me working with Maury, there was a whole crew of us in the Pine Street Irregulars helping him investigate. It was a varied group of about 8 to 10 people, some of whom were retired law enforcement.

The original Pine Street Irregulars were mostly friends of Maury's, local and federal law enforcement, and Yonkers locals. I knew that the group included about 10 people but only knew the identity of 3 of them. After Maury's death, I was able to identify a few more. Even today, I have not been able to identify all of them.

In 2016, I took it upon myself to form a new inner circle group of researchers. Because I do not know the true identities of a lot of the members, I had to be very selective as to who I let in the group. The number has ranged from as many as 10, was narrowed down to 4 and now stands at myself and one other. There are still members who help out, but I am always cautious sharing info, asking questions, and sceptical of "new" information I receive. A lot of times I receive information as facts, but when I delve into the info, it turns out to be assumptions and opinions. This information may be true but still needs a deeper dive into where the info came from.

I was recently asked to participate in a documentary on Maury and the Son of Sam case that is being directed by Josh Zeman and is to air on Netflix in 2021. When Josh asked me on camera if Maury had helped or hindered the case, I told him that no one should ever forget all the amazing work Maury had done bringing the case to public eye. But that being said, he did hinder the case. If he shared real information and real names, we might have been able to do something.

When it came to the new version of the book, he said he was going to take out some of the old information and add updated info; but when I saw the book, it was hard to see what he actually had changed. After his death, he put the book in the hands of Charles, a childhood friend of Maury's who didn't know anything about the case, as opposed to one of the people he had been working with for years, which was a wasted opportunity. In my opinion, he did a disservice to me as a victim and as an investigator. Other people and I had put in hundreds of hours on this case over the years. After his death, we were left with a ship with no captain. Then, I had to try and figure out things he knew but he never wrote them down. I've spent years just trying to figure out some people's real names.

He turned all his files over to Josh Zeman so he could do his documentary. I understand this. I am not a producer, I don't have any connections, so Josh has a better shot at doing the documentary than I ever could. I get that. But he didn't even give me permission to have full access to the files so I could look at them and possibly solve the case.

Over the years, he did a lot of good work keeping the story in the news, but we needed more than just circumstantial evidence. Unless Berkowitz and/or someone else comes forward corroborating his story, this case might never be officially solved.

There were rumours in the true crime world that Maury was stretching the truth. When you read *The Ultimate Evil*, it often seemed like he would make things up to make his points easier to believe.

There were, in theory, two prisoners in Attica that Maury said Berkowitz would talk to who then fed information to Maury. A lot of people said this wasn't true, that Maury was getting the information from Berkowitz, but it just sounded better if he said he had prison informants. There were also a lot of conversations in the book that were produced verbatim when it was obvious there was no way Maury would have the recall to remember them word for word.

Maury told me that when he was in high school he played in a band and was a songwriter who sold 10 of his original songs, including the classic pop song *Red Rubber Ball*. He told me received a check for $40k for writing these songs but he was not credited as a writer.

Maury told me the story about selling 10 songs for $40K several times and he also shared the story with several other people. Besides *Red Rubber Ball*, two of the other songs became hits. Maury did not like talking about this topic; if he had kept the writing credit, he would have been a millionaire. I always forgot the titles of the other two songs, but he wouldn't talk about it until he was pretty well lit. So on our monthly Friday night meetings at Kennedy's, I would ask again about the names of the two hits he wrote, but I would wait until 1 or 2 A.M. Unfortunately, I was also drinking and would wake up the next morning and couldn't remember the names of the songs. This happened several times.

It was probably not the best time to find out once and for all, but I asked anyway. At Maury's funeral, I approached his dad and introduced myself. I then apologized for the untimely question, "Did Maury write *Red Rubber Ball?*" His answer was something like this... "Yes, he did, but the idiot didn't retain the writing credits." I was a little flabbergasted by his remark and I forgot to ask him about the other two songs.

I don't think Maury's father would lie about this especially at his funeral. You can research *Red Rubber Ball* and never see a mention of Maury as the writer. In fact, the writer of the song is credited as Paul Simon; but back in the 1960s, producers at the Brill Building bought songs on a daily basis.

As I write this, my thoughts about Maury are mixed. I am still grieving over losing a friend, but in the meantime, I am also grieving the friend I thought he was.

I was able to mourn the loss of my friend, advocate, and mentor for a while. Once I got back to work on the case and started reaching out to some of the Facebook group members I could trust, a different picture started to emerge. When it became obvious that Maury wasn't always honest with me and others about the information he knew and even what he told us to research, I felt betrayed and played for a fool.

I think that Maury acted in this manner to keep the researchers working on the case, but to ensure only he knew the total picture so it could only be him that could re-open the case or submit info to the authorities. In the end, I think Maury actually hindered the re-opening of the case or, at the least, putting the information out there so victims and victims' families could initiate a civil case because of an incomplete investigation.

Afterword

This book has been forty years in the making. By 1978, after Berkowitz pled guilty to all charges and was sentenced, many of the Son of Sam stories had subsided in the daily newspapers. But interest in the case never totally waned. The Son of Sam murders continue to hold the public's fascination.

I attempted to lead a normal life after the shooting. I never went into the Air Force, for obvious reasons. Instead I got a job working for CitiCorp Center as the truck dock supervisor. I was making a decent salary. The job allowed me the luxury of getting my own apartment, driving my own car, and gave me enough spending money so I could hang out with my friends on occasion.

Unfortunately, wherever I went I was recognized as the guy that was shot by the Son of Sam. That doesn't sound like a big deal, but at the time in New York City, it certainly was. Imagine walking into a crowded bar, and before you could even order a drink, the noisy bar room chatter becoming a deafening silence. Everywhere I went, I could hear people whispering, "That's the guy that was shot by the Son of Sam."

I have a bit of an ego, and, my personality just naturally loves attention, but this was way out of my league. The notoriety became a real burden on my social life. It got to the point that I felt that I was losing my identity. I decided to quit my job, give up my apartment and get rid of all my belongings, and move to Friendswood, Texas to get away from the maddening crowd and, to a lesser extent, to get away from myself.

I packed my never-used Air Force duffel bag with my clothes and flew to Houston, Texas. While it was great to get away from the scrutiny of Queens, I missed my friends, my family, and my neighborhood. Friendswood, Texas is a very small town located about 30 miles south of Houston. Some of my friends were working construction there, so I knew I had a place to stay and I knew I had a job. On my second day in Texas, I ventured out for a walk to the local 7-Eleven, which was about a mile away, to get a 6-pack of beer. Much to my chagrin, apparently, I lived in a dry town and alcohol was not available. That wasn't going to fly with me. Needless to say, my stay in Texas lasted about 3 months.

Two of my friends, Pete and Marty, were driving to California to visit my old New York roommate, Bob O'Neill. I begged these guys to stop in Texas and get me out of there. Small town Texas living wasn't for me. The three of us arrived in Long Beach, California two days later. Belmont Shores, an upscale beach community at the southern end of Long Beach, would be my home for the next twenty months. My apartment was three blocks from the beach, it was summer all year long, and a few friends from Queens were also living there so it felt like home. I have great memories of my time in California, it was just what I needed to get my head straight. Sometimes a geographical cure works, no matter what people say.

After about a year in California, my lawyer contacted me, stating there was going to be a civil hearing for disbursement of Son of Sam funds to victims. He asked if I could possibly be in New York on January 2, 1980. I planned a 10-day vacation at Christmastime to visit family and friends and attend the hearing. After a few days in New York, I realized it was time to come home. California was beautiful, but I am a New York guy in my heart and in my soul.

I attended the hearing on January 2, 1980, at which time my lawyer for the civil lawsuit against David Berkowitz, Leland Sills, suggested I write a book about my experience. Forty years later, that is exactly what I am doing.

As previously mentioned in the book, while at the hearing, I heard lawyer Harry Lipsig, who was representing Robert Violante, badgering the judge, stating that other people were involved in the Son of Sam shootings. I had never heard this idea before and questioned my lawyer about it. He explained to me that information had become available and was recently presented to John Santucci's office, who was the Queens DA at the time. This information theorized that several people, in addition to David Berkowitz, were involved in the Son of Sam shootings.

The hearing was to determine monetary percentages due to victims based on their injury. As the hearing progressed, I learned that I was entitled to 2% of any monies made. At the time, David Berkowitz had a net worth of approximately $120,000. My percentage amounted to approximately $2,400. I have to say getting shot in the head is a tough way to make $2,400. I definitely don't recommend it. After the hearing was over, I flew back to California, and then moved back to New York permanently in April of 1980. I came back to New York in May of 1980 and, as luck would have it, the 2% of the monetary award I was set to receive arrived shortly thereafter, which enabled me to get an apartment and furnish it.

During this time, my lawyer brought up writing a book again. I told him I might be able to write a chapter of a book about my experience, but there is no way anyone would want to read more than a chapter because I didn't have much information to share above and beyond what I read in the papers. Decades later, that is no longer true.

As far as how I am these days, I know I am a lucky guy to survive a .44 bullet to my head and am grateful for every day I am alive. With that said, I am not complaining, but not a day goes by that I am not reminded of being shot.

The lasting effects are minor, but I think worth noting. My middle finger on my right hand is permanently bent at the top knuckle due to the tendon being sliced by a bullet fragment. It doesn't hurt but goes numb when the winters of New York City come around.

I have a loss of vision below my waist on my right side. This disability does not hurt at all but has proven troublesome over the years. I have injured myself several times walking into fire hydrants, bike racks, and garbage cans. I have learned to walk with my head down so I can see objects that I wouldn't see looking straight ahead. I have had this vision issue since I was shot, but I didn't really know what was going on. I was always curious as to how I would just be walking along and bang right into a fire hydrant. When I was in my 40s, I was having trouble reading books, menus, labels, and things of that nature, so I went to the optometrist. One of the tests I took showed me clearly what was wrong. I was told to look into a black screen and press a button whenever I saw a flash of light. When I saw the results, the entire screen was filled with dots except for the lower right quadrant, it was completely blank. The mystery was solved. I'm not clumsy, I can't see!

The back of my head where the plate was inserted is still tender and painful to the touch. I hate getting my hair cut because of this. Brushing my hair back with a brush is a carefully planned and executed chore. When taking a shower, the water hitting my head sounds like water hitting a tin roof inside my head. It is annoying but not painful unless the water hits the back of my head directly. It is a very strange feeling and a constant reminder of my injury.

I know I made the right decision to leave New York when I did. I also know I made the right decision to come back to New York. I had to leave when I did for the sake of my sanity, but when I came back, there was almost no talk of the Son of Sam. The whole saga had clearly dissipated. Life seemed pretty much back to normal.

That all changed in 1987, when Maury Terry's book was published. All of a sudden, I was in the spotlight all over again.

This book is my attempt to not only present the evidence that Maury, myself, and other investigators have come up with since *The Ultimate Evil* was published. It's also my attempt to come to terms with two things that have had an enormous effect on my life.

One is that I was not only shot in the head in one of the most famous criminal cases in the history of this country, but I still don't know with absolute certainty who shot me. Although, I am sure it wasn't David Berkowitz.

The other thing that affected my life enormously was my friendship, and subsequent work as an investigator with Maury Terry. He was a complicated man, and one who let me down in certain ways. He was also an incredible person and I miss him dearly.

Cast of Characters

There is a lot of information in this book, but there is some that was not included, purely because it wasn't crucial to the overall narrative. For those of you who have followed this case from the beginning as well as those of you who are new to the case and want to know more, I have put together a list of the known and suspected participants of the Son of Sam saga.

As I mentioned previously, I am only naming the real names of suspects who have already been named by Maury Terry or others. I have included some names that are pseudonyms in this cast of characters to help readers follow along.

The case is not solved and without people in the know coming forward, it probably will never be solved.

This list is by no means complete. Some names associated with the case have been left off the list because I do not know much about them. I have used the information the Pine Street Irregulars with Maury leading the charge, my own research, input from the members of the Official Maury Terry – "The Ultimate Evil" – Son of Sam & Beyond Facebook group and, for a few years, a small but determined research group I was lucky enough to be part of.

If you would like to get involved and share your information on the Son of Sam case or want to investigate any of the names listed...here is your chance!

I will soon have a secure website where all members will be screened and vetted. For now, please send any questions, concerns, and information to my email: CarlDenaroSOSsurvivor@gmail.com

SUSPECTS

First Attack

Shooter

David Berkowitz

Accomplices

Gorman Johnson and "Richie" who were in the tan getaway car.

Michael Carr was the driver of the light yellow car seen cruising the neighborhood earlier in the evening.

Second Attack

Shooter

NYPD claims it was David Berkowitz.

Berkowitz claims it is a woman, which is backed up by NYPD ballistics Det. Quirk.

Maury and Pine Street Irregulars claim it is either a woman named Amy or Wendy who is a known occult priestess who might also be the same person known as "big breasted Wendy".

Accomplice

None that I am aware of, although David Berkowitz has stated that multiple accomplices were at all of the attacks.

Third Attack

Shooter

The NYPD says it was David Berkowitz even though the sketches they released of the shooter very closely resemble John Carr. Both victims described the shooter as 5 ft 9 inches tall, slender and blond which closely resembles John Carr.

Both David Berkowitz and Maury Terry say the shooter was John Carr.

Accomplice

David Berkowitz

Fourth Attack

Shooter

NYPD says the shooter was David Berkowitz

Maury Terry says the shooter was Bill Mentzer aka Manson II who is currently serving prison time in California for the murder of Roy Radin. David Berkowitz has admitted that the shooter was brought in from the West Coast but did not name the shooter.

Accomplice

David Berkowitz

Fifth Attack

Shooter

The NYPD says the shooter was David Berkowitz, although they stated that the person in the ski cap was a prime suspect.

Accomplices

David Berkowitz and another whose name is unknown to me. The NYPD were looking for a white male, 6 feet tall, with black hair combed straight back.

Sixth Attack

Shooter

David Berkowitz

Accomplice

None that I am aware of, although David Berkowitz has stated that multiple accomplices were at all of the attacks.

Seventh Attack

Shooter

NYPD says it was David Berkowitz.

Both David Berkowitz and Maury Terry say it was Michael Carr.

Accomplices

David Berkowitz and Gorman Johnson driving a tan getaway car.

Eighth Attack

Shooter

NYPD says it was David Berkowitz.

Maury Terry says it was Larry Lomenko.

Accomplices

David Berkowitz, whose Ford Galaxy was ticketed at 2 A.M. on the opposite side of the park.

There were three accomplices in a VW Microbus filming the attack. Ronald Sisman and two others, one of whom was possibly a woman, based on eyewitness accounts.

Additional Information on Some of the Players

Berkowitz, David One of the 22 Disciples of Hell referred to in the Breslin letter. Berkowitz murdered 3 people and wounded one. He was present at all of the attacks.

Billy The Artist - Real name not known. He witnessed Satanic rituals in Untermeyer Park and sketched some of the participants.

Brother John- Deceased. He was an early Process Church member who left the cult in 1970. In the 1960's, he was molested as a teenager at Untermeyer Park, and soon after that was trafficked for sexual purposes to rich clients in Manhattan. He was also involved in the Greenwich Village Stonewall riots. His interview at the 25th anniversary of the Stonewall riots can be found on the internet. He left New York and moved to Milwaukee as a street preacher, eventually ministering to Jeffrey Dahmer.

Caan, Jimmy Allegedly one of the 22 Disciples of Hell, but he was not at any of the Son of Sam attacks. He lived in the apartment building at 35 Pine Street, Yonkers N.Y. The same building as David Berkowitz. David Berkowitz has stated in interviews that they were friends and accomplices. Caan was one of several people who helped clear out and deface Berkowitz's apartment days before his arrest to make it look like a madman lived there. Caan committed suicide right after the Yonkers Police Department questioned him about the Son of Sam case when the case was reopened in the mid-1990's.

Carr, John– Deceased. He was allegedly one of the 22 Disciples of Hell referred to in the Breslin letter. Was almost certainly a shooter in the third attack.

Carr, Michael -Deceased. He was allegedly one of the 22 Disciples of Hell referred to in the Breslin letter. Was one of the core cult members.

Carr, Sam- Father of John, Michael, and Wheat. Owner of the infamous black Lab, "Harvey".

Carozza, Alphonse -Allegedly one of the 22 Disciples of Hell. He was murdered on his yacht, the SARC, on New Year's Eve, 1981. Prison source, "Vinny", had warned Maury that the Son of Sam cult had a target hit slated for December 31, 1981 two months before Carozza was gunned down. Carozza had had close ties to a person who lived at 22 Wicker Street and it was speculated by Yonkers Detectives that he might be The Wicked King that Wicker referred to in the Breslin letter.

Cassara, Sam-Worked at the Neptune Moving Company in Yonkers with Fred Cowen and Robert Mapplethorpe. He was David Berkowitz's landlord prior to Berkowitz moving to 35 Pine Street in Yonkers, N.Y.

Chase, Lee-Within days of Berkowitz's arrest, she somehow became his confidante. A known born-again Christian from the Midwest, she persuaded Berkowitz to plead guilty to all shootings. I am not really sure how she even got access to him.

Conway, Susan-Deceased. Allegedly one of the 22 Disciples of Hell referred to in the Breslin letter. Maury described her as "the wasted-from-drugs priestess."

Cowan, Fred-Neo Nazi who shot 8 people at the Neptune Moving Company in Yonkers. David Berkowitz has admitted that he knew him. Cowan worked with Sam Cassara and John Mapplethorpe at Neptune Moving Company

"Danny" - Maury Terry's prison informant. I have not been able to identify Danny's real name.

Dorfler, Aileen-Close friend or relative of Wheat Carr. Dorfler's sister owned a home on 156th Street in Flushing, which was blocks away from the Denaro/Keenan attack making it a possible meeting point for the shooting. She was the mother of Glenn Dorfler.

Dorfler, Glenn-Deceased. Worked for Jim Faulkner in a recording studio. Son of Aileen Dorfler. Wheat Carr posted a message after his death referring to him as her nephew.

Duece- Pimp who operated out of Manhattan's 42nd Street area who procured teens, mostly boys, for the elite in Manhattan and Yonkers.

Faulkner, James- Former NYPD cop fired from force after a road rage incident where he fired two shots into the air while driving his VW bug. He doesn't remember the color of the VW bug. Although he lost his NYPD job, his lawyer dragged the case through the courts for two years and the case was eventually dropped due to the fact he didn't get a fair and speedy trial. Good friends with Wheat Carr, he eventually bought the Carr house for below market value. Several years ago, there was major excavation around and behind the Carr house. Six months later, the house was in foreclosure. Yonkers Police were notified of the excavation. Nothing came of it. Makes you wonder what he was looking for???

Gajdusek, Carleton-Deceased. Nobel Prize winner. Convicted Pedophile. "Adopted" over 30 young boys from Micronesia and brought them to the US. It was one of the boys who accused the good doctor of abusing him. Maintained a house in Maryland and one in Yonkers. His connection to the Son of Sam case is not very clear, but one thing is clear; he is another pedophile with ties to Yonkers.

Harvey-Sam Carr's pet black Lab. Harvey was shot by a .38, allegedly by David Berkowitz, but survived. Spike Lee used a stand-in for Harvey during the "talking dog" scene in his "Summer of Sam" movie.

Hauser, William- Man who slashed the throat of David Berkowitz in prison, although he was never charged with the crime, in theory because Berkowitz was too frightened to cooperate. He is currently incarcerated for beating a man to death with a rolling pin.

Howell, Alfred-Alternative suspect raised by another researcher whose real name is not known to me. One of two people suspected of being Mr. Real Estate. Mr. Real Estate is suspected of being the mastermind behind the Son of Sam attacks.

Johnson, Gorman- lived across the street from 35 Pine Street, Yonkers. Now deceased, he was a teacher in Yonkers. Early in his life he drove a taxi for the Co-Op City Taxi Company who also employed David Berkowitz. Interestingly, he was interviewed on TV twice, once for a story on the Yonkers Dart Man and later a Son of Sam story.

Ken From Australia-Process Church member - Allegedly one of the 22 Disciples of Hell referred to in the Breslin letter. Dated Yvette Rodriguez and sketched by "The Artist" during rituals in Untermeyer Park.

Mapplethorpe, Robert-A known Satanist. He allegedly approached Jesse Turner to set up the murder of Ron Sisman and Elizabeth Platzman. According to the authorized documentary on his life, he would visit his parents' home at all hours. The home is on 259th Street in Floral Park, Queens, a mere 3 blocks away from the Lomino/DiMasi shooting. David Berkowitz's sister lived in Glen Oaks and he has stated in interviews that he visited regularly in 1976 and 1977. Glen Oaks is about 15 blocks away from the Lomino/DiMasi shooting. Allegedly worked at Neptune Moving Company along with Fred Cowen and Sam Cassara.

McCabe, John-Was married to Wheat Carr in the 1970's. He was a Yonkers cop that was fired from the force for unknown reasons. No records can be found about his dismissal. Maury once told me that McCabe said he was involved in some bad stuff and had to marry Wheat.

Menter, William AKA Manson 11(as per Maury Terry) - currently serving prison time in California for the murder of Roy Radin. Suspected shooter in Christine Freund attack.

Milenko, Larry[4] Allegedly brought in from the Midwest to be the triggerman at the 8th and final

---

4. Pseudonym

SOS attack of Violante/Moskowitz. He had a prior arrest for running a meth lab and was sentenced to 5 years. Suspected in the murder/accidental death of Jerry Berg in Minot, N.D. Currently involved in a bio-dome project in North Carolina.

Mr. Real Estate-, the leader of the cult. He was also identified as Moloch, and the mastermind behind the Son of Sam attacks.

Quinn, Peter- deceased - Allegedly one of the 22 Disciples of Hell referred to in the Breslin letter. Described as a drugged-out dog killer and arsonist.

Radin, Roy-Vaudeville promoter who became a millionaire at an early age. Held lavish parties in his Hamptons mansion which reportedly included wild drug and sex parties. Was arrested for the Melanie Haller incident and eventually got in too deep on the West Coast trying to break into the movie business with Robert Evan's, *Cotton Club*. He was also involved with large drug shipments with Laine Jakobs. He was murdered with a bullet to the back of his head. William "Bill" Mentzer is serving time in a California prison for his murder.

"Richie" - A friend of David Berkowitz who was an accomplice during at least one shooting attack.

Rockman, Reeve - Reeve Rockman is chronicled in *The Ultimate Evil*.

Rodriguez, Suzette-AKA Maria Cortina-Allegedly one of the 22 Disciples of Hell referred to in the Breslin letter. Dated Ken Naughton (Process Church member). Sketched by "The Artist" during rituals in Untermeyer Park.

Rothstein, Jim-Retired NYPD detective who worked the 42nd street area. So many runaways from America's heartland were arriving on buses by the droves in the 1970's. Rothstein was given the job to help these runaways before the pimps got to them. His sources led him to teen prostitution and trafficking from 42nd Street to Untermeyer Park in Yonkers. He was the first law enforcement official to find and report on these activities along with the Satanic rituals that were being held in the park in 1970, six years before the Son of Sam attacks.

Santucci, John-Queens District Attorney. Re-opened the Son of Sam case in 1980. The investigation was shut down 6 weeks later.

Scout-Allegedly one of the 22 Disciples of Hell referred to in the Breslin letter. Arrested at 17 years old for sodomizing several young boys. Scout was friends with John Carr as early as 1961 when they were both in high school. Even at this early age, people knew that both Scout and Carr were "into witchcraft" and, apparently, sodomy.

Shane, Peter[5] Allegedly one of the 22 Disciples of Hell referred to in the Breslin letter. He was also an officer in the Yonkers PD.

Sisman, Ron-Photographer, videographer, and drug dealer. Friends with Roy Radin. Allegedly was one of the 3 men in the VW bus filming the Violante/Moskowitz shooting. Sisman was also involved in the Melanie Haller sexual abuse case. Haller was found on the Long Island Railroad heading into Manhattan from The Hamptons in Eastern Long Island. The abuse apparently happened in Roy Radin's mansion.

Spero, Mike-NYPD officer - NYPD considered him a suspect. He owned a yellow VW that had

5. Pseudonym

vanity plates GRK-44. His photo matches one of the nine police sketches,

Tacco-Allegedly one of the 22 Disciples of Hell referred to in the Breslin letter. Convicted and registered as a pedophile. It is believed that he was David Berkowitz's "boss". Currently living in South Carolina.

Turner, Jesse-A bank robber who was an associate of the Process Church and the occult scene in New York. Shared an apartment with Robert Mapplethorpe and Patti Smith for a year or so. Allegedly, Mapplethorpe asked Turner to get the snuff film that Ron Sisman had and then kill him. Jesse became a valuable source unlocking many questions in the Son of Sam case. Short clips of him talking about the case can be found on the internet.

"Vinny" - Maury Terry's prison informant. I have not been able to identify Vinny's real name

Acknowledgments

I wouldn't have been able to start or finish this book without the groundbreaking investigation by the late Maury Terry. In 1985 Maury laid out the groundwork of this complicated case and continued to keep the Son of Sam case in the public eye. Rest in Peace Maury.

I will always be indebted to my daughter Casey, for making me realize I really did have a story to tell and followed up her faith in me by enrolling me in writing classes and encouraging me throughout this project.

Thank you, Brian Whitney, my cowriter, who molded my thoughts and rambling stories into a cohesive story. Without you guiding me through the book writing process I would still be working on Chapter two.

My appreciation is also extended to the staff at Wild Blue Press including Michael Cordova, Steve Jackson, Ashley Kaesemeyer, and Natalie DeYoung.

Chip MacGregor, principal at the MacGregor Literary Agency who jumped on board with the project and continues to guide and assist in making my book a success.

I am grateful to Josh Zemen for reaching out to me shortly after Maury's passing to discuss the future of Maury Terry's "The Ultimate Evil" estate. A huge thank you to Caitlin Colford for her assistance, fact checking dates and time lines ensuring accuracy of the historical facts of the case.

Thanks to author, Susan Fensten for introducing me to Brian Whitney.

To all the members of Facebook groups, The Official Maury Terry-"The Ultimate Evil" – Son of Sam & Beyond Group and The Unofficial Maury Terry –"The Ultimate Evil Group" who have contributed their time and resources investigating the Son of Sam story.

Special thanks to the independent researchers who continue to Investigate and keep me updated with their findings including Howie E., Jessica D., Don R., and Tomac. Thanks to all of the researchers who have helped me in the past who are too numerous to name.

Finally, my gratitude to my girlfriend, Trish Scida, who transcribed a large portion of the book and more importantly, became my sounding board and confidante during the book writing process. Her patience with me went above and beyond! Thanks!

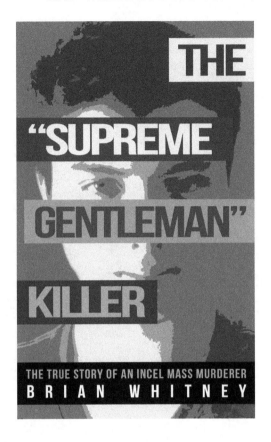

**AVAILABLE FROM MARY BRETT
AND WILDBLUE PRESS!**

OUT OF THE MOUTHS OF SERIAL
KILLERS by MARY BRETT

http://wbp.bz/mouthsserialkillersa